THE BLOODY CROSSROADS

Where Literature and Politics Meet

Norman Podhoretz

SIMON AND SCHUSTER   NEW YORK

All of the articles in this book have been previously published.

Published by Simon and Schuster
A Division of Simon & Schuster, Inc.
Simon & Schuster Building
Rockefeller Center
1230 Avenue of the Americas
New York, New York 10020
SIMON AND SCHUSTER and colophon are registered trademarks
of Simon & Schuster, Inc.

Designed by Helen L. Granger/Levavi & Levavi
Manufactured in the United States of America

10 9 8 7 6 5 4 3 2 1

Library of Congress Cataloging-in-Publication Data
Podhoretz, Norman.
    The bloody crossroads.

    Includes index.
    Contents: Why The god that failed failed—Camus and
his critics—If Orwell were alive today—[etc.]
    1. Politics and literature—Addresses, essays,
lectures. 2. Communism and literature—Addresses,
essays, lectures. I. Title.
PN51.P54 1986   814'.54   85-27908
ISBN: 0-671-61891-1

ACKNOWLEDGMENTS

"The Adversary Culture and the New Class" is reprinted by permission and first appeared in a volume edited by B. Bruce-Briggs under the title *The New Class?* (New Brunswick, Transaction Press, 1979; copyright 1979 Center for Policy Research). "Why *The God That Failed* Failed" was written as the introduction to a new Gateway paperback edition of that book and first appeared in *Encounter*. "If Orwell Were Alive Today" first appeared in *Harper's*. My thanks to all the editors and publishers involved for permission to reprint.

I am especially grateful to Hilton Kramer, the editor of *The New Criterion,* who commissioned the essays on Leavis, Camus, and Adams, for encouraging me to begin writing on such subjects again. And, as ever, I owe an enormous debt to Neal Kozodoy, and to Brenda Brown and Marion Magid, my other colleagues on the staff of *Commentary,* in which the essays on Kissinger, Kundera, and Solzhenitsyn were originally published.

Finally, I want to thank my son, John Podhoretz, for persuading me to put this collection together.

I should add that for the purposes of this book, the only revisions I made beyond the merely cosmetic were a matter of eliminating outdated references or minimizing the inevitable overlap between different essays.

For Huw Wheldon

CONTENTS

INTRODUCTION

The essays collected here were written separately—all except one since 1982—but they have, I believe, so much in
common that they belong together in a single volume.

To begin with, they all deal with authors who stand (in
the phrase I have taken from Lionel Trilling for my title)
at "the bloody crossroads where literature and politics meet."
Why bloody? Because, as I once said in trying to explain
what Trilling meant, "blood has often actually been shed
in the clash between literature and politics. Writers have
been killed by politicians for expressing certain ideas or
writing in certain ways; but (what is less often acknowledged) these same politicians have also been inspired by
other writers to shed the blood of their fellow writers, and
millions of nonwriters as well."

But that is perhaps too general, either as a gloss on Trilling or as a description of the main theme of this book. For

as the name of Anthony Trollope alone reminds us, the intersection of literature and politics has not always been marked in blood. Nor, as we are reminded by such golden ages of literature as sixteenth-century England and nineteenth-century Russia, has there always been literary blood on the hands of traditional tyrannies. It is not, then, politics alone, nor even the politics of despotism and tyranny, that literature runs into so violently at the bloody crossroads; it is totalitarianism, the twentieth century's distinctive contribution to despotism and tyranny.

And yet even that is too general a statement of the case. For of the two major forms of totalitarianism, Communism has come into much bloodier contact with literature than fascism even at its Nazi worst. Hitler, of course, burned books and persecuted writers at home, just as Stalin did, and he was in a sense more directly guided by Nietzsche than Stalin was by Marx. But unlike Stalin, and Lenin before him, Hitler inspired very few writers abroad to apologize for his crimes against their fellow writers, let alone his crimes against any other groups or classes. With the obvious exceptions of Ezra Pound, Wyndham Lewis, Louis-Ferdinand Céline, and a few others, mostly French and now mostly forgotten, even those writers in the democracies who to a greater or lesser degree sympathized with fascism rarely did so with the kind of wholehearted enthusiasm that countless writers have from the beginning felt and openly displayed for Communism.

Accordingly, the politics most often found at the bloody crossroads is Communism. Accordingly, too, the second feature most of the essays collected here have in common is a preoccupation with Communism, especially as it is embodied in the Soviet Union, the most powerful of all the Communist states.

Third, and narrowing the focus still further, most of the

writers I discuss (the exceptions in this instance include Henry Adams, F. R. Leavis, and Henry Kissinger) are former Communists driven by the compulsion to warn the democratic world against the threat of an evil that few of them would hesitate to describe as absolute. Yet on the whole these ex-Communists are no more enthusiastic about the democratic world, especially as embodied in the United States, the most powerful of all the democracies, than are Adams and Leavis and the many like-minded intellectuals whose attitudes are analyzed in "The Adversary Culture and the New Class."

One of my purposes in this book is to explore the literary roots of such attitudes toward the United States, and to suggest why they are as misguided as they are dangerous. Another of my purposes, implicit throughout and explicit in the essay on Kissinger, is to show that the testimony of the ex-Communists makes nonsense of the hopes for peaceful coexistence, or détente, between the two systems. Neither, however, does it make war inevitable—a point I have argued in a number of essays not included in this collection because they are strictly and entirely political.

Which brings me to the fourth element the essays that are included in this collection have in common: they are all (even the one on Kissinger, who is here primarily as an author and not as a statesman) either pieces of literary criticism or of literary and cultural history. They thus represent an attempt to merge the political issues that have largely concerned me as a writer during the past twenty years with my originally overriding interest in literature.

It is no secret that I have changed my mind about many things since the days when I wrote mostly about literature. But about some things I have not changed my mind at all. I still believe now, as I did in the late fifties and early sixties, that it is possible for a critic to speak openly from a particular political perspective and to make political judgments without permitting such judgments to replace or obscure literary values as such. I still believe (see "Henry Adams: The 'Powerless' Intellectual in America") that it is possible to recognize and acknowledge the literary power of a writer and at the same time to dislike or even loathe his work on political grounds. I still believe, conversely (see "The Terrible Question of Aleksandr Solzhenitsyn"), that one can admire and even revere a writer while recognizing and acknowledging the aesthetic weaknesses of his work.

In short, I believe that a critic can talk about literature in a way that respects its autonomy without denying or suppressing a concern with other values, and most of all without attributing literary virtues to bad books because they are on the "right" (which nowadays, of course, usually means the Left) political side, or attacking a good book on literary grounds when the real objection is to its politics.

I am well aware that these formulations do not begin to do justice to the complicated relation between literature and politics. But perhaps they will at least serve as a signpost pointing the way toward the bloody crossroads in which the essays that follow, like the writers with whom they deal, all find themselves forced by history to stand.

PART ONE

The God That Failed

1.

WHY *THE GOD THAT FAILED* FAILED

I was only about twenty years old, a senior in college, the first time I read *The God That Failed,* and I can still remember how dazzled and exhilarated it left me feeling. There are books of my youth that I have returned to in later life only to be disappointed or even mystified at the effect they once had on me. *The God That Failed* has not proved to be one of these books. Rereading it today, I can see easily enough why it should once have exerted so powerful an influence on my thinking about Communism. But today I can also see portents that were invisible to me then of problems that were to bedevil and confuse the discussion of Communism in the decades ahead. The full emergence of these problems in the 1980s is what adds a touch of poignancy to *The God That Failed* for someone like myself who first encountered it in the early 1950s. But it is also what makes this book more than merely a historical curiosity for the reader who is coming upon it for the first time today.

To understand the power and influence of *The God That Failed* when it was originally published, it is necessary to bear in mind that Communism in those early days of the cold war was the single most salient issue of political concern throughout the Western world. This had by no means been the case in the period immediately preceding the outbreak of the cold war. From the mid-1930s until the mid-1940s, the Soviet Union itself and the Communist parties in other countries (all of which were then under the direct control of Moscow) had done everything they could to blur the distinction between Communism on the one side and democratic socialism or liberalism on the other. In a still earlier phase, Communists had had nothing but contempt for "bourgeois" liberals and their values and had professed to see no difference between fascists and democratic socialists. But in response to the threat posed by the rise of Hitler in Germany, the Soviet Union under Stalin thought it the better part of prudence to seek alliances with the formerly despised bourgeois democracies. At that point, Communists everywhere suddenly changed their "line" and began representing themselves as "liberals in a hurry"—that is, people who differed from New Deal Democrats in the United States (or supporters of the various socialist parties in other countries who had previously been regarded by the Communists as "social fascists") only in the degree of their zealous impatience for the creation of a better world.

During the Second World War, the Communists were if anything even more eager to blur the distinction between democracy and Communism in the interests of the Soviet alliance with the Western democracies against the fascist powers. It was only in the postwar period that the line changed once again in the direction of revolutionary militancy, carrying in its train a renewed hostility toward "bour-geois" liberalism and democratic socialism.

Thanks to these many twists and turns, the discussion of the Soviet Union and of Communism (the two were still interchangeable) had been thoroughly corrupted by men-dacity on the one side and naiveté or credulousness on the other. It was into the resultant intellectual darkness that a series of flares was fired, of which *The God That Failed* was one of the brightest (two others being Hannah Arendt's *The Origins of Totalitarianism* and Whittaker Chambers's *Witness*).

In one way or another, all these books attempted to show that Communism had more in common with Nazism and fascism than with liberalism or democratic socialism. This being the case, with the defeat of Nazi Germany in World War II, the Soviet Union had emerged as the single greatest threat on earth to the democratic values it had so recently professed to have realized much more fully than the West-ern democracies themselves, and which it had claimed to be fighting for against Hitler and his allies.

Indeed, from the point of view of most of these writers, Communism was more dangerous than Nazism or fascism precisely because it exerted a much greater ideological ap-peal. Nazism frankly and nakedly set itself against all democratic values, preaching doctrines such as the innate in-feriority of non-"Aryan" races that were inherently repug-nant to anyone raised in the traditions of the West. Hence its power rested mainly on brute force and could be success-fully resisted by force alone. Communism was subtler and more insidious. It had come into the world, it said, not to repeal the liberal democratic order but to fulfill it. At vari-ous moments the Communists might openly acknowledge that this fulfillment could be achieved only by a violent overthrow of the existing system; or for tactical reasons they might pretend to believe that it could be achieved peacefully and without recourse to revolution. But whatever the means advocated, the end envisioned was a world in which the liberal democratic order would supposedly be brought to a higher stage of development and finally perfected by the abolition of capitalism and its attendant inequalities and injustices.

For this reason, while Communism was no less dangerous to the body than Nazism or fascism—in the simple sense that it too rested on force and brutal repression—it was infinitely more dangerous to the mind. Therefore, it was particularly dangerous to people who lived the life of the mind—people to whom ideas and ideologies were meat and drink (or, in many cases, bread and wine). It was this which explained the paradoxical susceptibility of intellectuals to Communism. Paradoxical because intellectuals were accorded a position in the Communist scheme subordinate to that of the working class which—a correlative paradox— had on the whole been less susceptible to the appeal of Communism despite its placement at the very center of Communist theory.

The God That Failed set out to explore this paradox through accounts by six famous intellectuals of how and why they had become Communists (either actually joining the Communist party or acting as "fellow travelers"—that is, loyal supporters and apologists from outside) and how and why they had eventually broken with the party. All six were writers, but otherwise they varied widely in background. Arthur Koestler had come to England from Hungary by way of Austria and Germany, and was, by the time of *The God That Failed,* internationally famous both as a novelist and as a political analyst. Ignazio Silone was perhaps the best-known Italian novelist of the day, and Richard Wright enjoyed a comparable position among black American writers. André Gide's reputation is not so great today, but in 1950 he was widely regarded as the greatest living French novelist and perhaps the leading man of letters in the whole of Europe. Louis Fischer, the least considerable of the six even then and almost completely forgotten today, was in his time a major figure in the world of international journalism. Finally, there was Stephen Spender, a British poet and critic, also famous on both sides of the Atlantic. R. H. S. Crossman, who conceived the idea for *The God That Failed* in collaboration with Koestler and then wrote the introduction, was both an influential political journalist and an important figure in the Labour party.

I stress the fame and prestige of the authors of *The God That Failed* because these attributes were essential to the main effect the book had on me (and, I feel sure, on most of its original readers). It took a book like *The Origins of Totalitarianism* to refute the idea that Communism and Nazism stood at opposite ends of the political spectrum and to establish the theoretical case for seeing them both as totalitarian systems, embodiments of the most highly developed form of despotism known to human history, a despotism that embraced not merely the political sphere but every area of life. But it took a book like *The God That Failed,* with its rich collection of personal testimony from so many literary celebrities, to legitimate anti-Communism, to make it a respectable and even a mandatory political position within the American intellectual community, no less mandatory than anti-Nazism or antifascism had been in that community since the 1930s.

Of course the authors of *The God That Failed* were neither the first nor even necessarily the most prominent anti-Communist intellectuals in the West. Philosophers like Bertrand Russell in England and John Dewey in America had arrived at an anti-Communist position long before any

of the contributors to *The God That Failed* and without an
intervening period of commitment to Communism. But
when Koestler told Crossman that "we ex-Communists are
the only people . . . who know what it's about," or when
Silone said to the Italian Communist leader Togliatti that
the final battle would be between the Communists and the
ex-Communists, they were right in claiming a special intimate sense of the true nature of Communism usually ab-
sent from the writings of anti-Communists who had never
fallen victim to its wiles and allures.

That the ex-Communists were always being accused of
lying by their former friends and comrades went without
saying; and lying was the least of the accusations hurled at
these apostates from the true faith, who were shunned and
vilified, whose reputations were besmirched, and whose
characters were assassinated. But the ex-Communists were
even a little suspect in the eyes of other anti-Communists,
who were always accusing them of exaggerating or of over-
dramatizing. "You hate our Cassandra cries," Crossman
quotes Koestler as complaining to him, in the conversation
out of which the idea for *The God That Failed* was born.
Crossman with characteristic enthusiasm responded by challenging Koestler to tell his story, and as he listened, it suddenly occurred to him that "This should be a book." Evidently there was something the ex-Communists knew that
"all you comfortable, insular, Anglo-Saxon anti-Communists" (as Koestler called them) were unable to grasp. In
the end, Crossman was forced to acknowledge that Koestler
was right. "No one who has not wrestled with Communism
as a philosophy, and Communists as political opponents, can
really understand the values of Western democracy. The
Devil once lived in Heaven, and those who have not met
him are unlikely to recognize an angel when they see one."

What was it that these ex-Communists knew that an anti-

Communist like Richard Crossman did not really know? Obviously, the facts about the Soviet Union were as available to people who had never been Communists as they were to those who had. Anyone who took the trouble to look could see that the Soviet Union, far from being more democratic than the United States or the West European countries, was a society in the grip of a totalitarian system as thorough-going and as brutal as Nazi Germany. Anyone who took the trouble to look could see that there was no freedom of any kind there, and that even the value of equality—the prime value, after all, of Soviet political culture—had not been and was unlikely ever to be more fully realized in the Soviet Union than in the democratic world. Anyone who took the trouble to look could see that the economic prob-lems of capitalism and the sufferings they caused were mild as compared with the terrible poverty of Russia and the wholesale starvation and murder involved in the collectivi-zation of agriculture. Anyone who took the trouble to look could see that the Soviet Union, far from being the spear-head of a new internationalism in world affairs, and far from being the only reliable bulwark against fascism, would unhesitatingly betray the antifascist cause (as Stalin did in signing a pact with the Nazis in 1939) if it suited the crass national interests of the Soviet state. Anyone who took the trouble to look could see that, far from being the great op-ponent of imperialism, the Soviet Union was seizing on the opportunity presented by its military successes in the Second World War to establish a great new empire. Anyone who took the trouble to look could see that, far from being peace-loving, the Soviet Union was maintaining its armies at war-time strength and threatening to extend its imperial sway beyond the domains of Eastern Europe, which it was already ruling by force.

It is a fact, and a source of continual astonishment, that

many people neither knew nor saw these things. Some of these people were, of course, Communists or fellow travelers who had yet to encounter what Louis Fischer in his contribution to *The God That Failed* called their "Kronstadt" (that is, the episode that decisively shattered their illusions about the Soviet Union). But there were many others who were neither Communists nor fellow travelers in the strict sense of being ready to accept every twist and turn in the party line, and who were yet unable or unwilling to face the truth about the Soviet Union. Such people, who generally thought of themselves as liberals (a title to which they had no solid claim even though they successfully managed to identify themselves with it in their own eyes and the eyes of the media), adamantly refused to believe that the Soviet Union was as bad as it appeared to be or that Communists were anything more than "liberals in a hurry." Inclined always to give the Soviet Union the benefit of the doubt, ready always with an apologetic explanation for anything the Soviets did, they were equally ready to treat the Communists as participants, along with all other right-minded, decent, progressive people, in the struggle for social justice at home.

The point about these "liberals" is that they simply could not take Communism *seriously*. Even when the Communists themselves were no longer claiming that Communism was (as Earl Browder, the leader of the American Communist party once described it in the heyday of the Popular Front) "Twentieth-Century Americanism," these "liberals" persisted in their illusions. And even in the face of one "Kronstadt" after another—the bloody suppression by the Red Army of a sailors' revolt at Kronstadt itself in the early twenties; the murder of millions of peasants who resisted the collectivization of agriculture in the early thirties; the Stalinist purges and show trials of the mid-thirties; the Hitler-Stalin Pact of the late thirties; the establishment of Communist puppet regimes in East Europe in the forties—the same "liberals" went on denying that the Soviet Union was an expansionist totalitarian state with a closer resemblance to Nazi Germany than to any of the democracies of the West.

Nor were illusions about the Soviet Union to be found only among "liberals." A good many businessmen, who thought of themselves as "conservatives" and anti-Communists, nevertheless seized upon every opportunity to help the Soviet Union develop its industrial base. Without such help, it is unlikely that the Soviet Union would ever have grown into the military superpower it eventually became. If we ask ourselves how and why Western capitalists should have done all this, only part of the answer was the quest for profits (which, incidentally, usually turned out to be either illusory or disappointing). The other and perhaps more important part was the same refusal to take Communism seriously as an ideology or the Soviet Union seriously as an enemy that characterized the "liberal" attitude.

But to return to Richard Crossman, who unlike certain "liberals" *did* know the truth about the Soviet Union and unlike certain "conservatives" really *was* an anti-Communist—he had doubtless learned to take Communism seriously even though he had never been a Communist himself. Even so, there is a breeziness about his introduction to *The God That Failed* that belies his own characterization of Communism as the "Devil"; he writes in a tone that stands in very sharp contrast indeed to the tone in which the six ex-Communists in the book talk about the issue. One can see why Koestler accused Crossman of being "comfortable" and "insular." Crossman could explain Communism; he could recognize what was wrong with it; and he could analyze its appeal. But what he was unable to do was to convey a sense of the urgency and magnitude of the struggle against Communism. For this the ex-Communists, with their "Cassandra cries," were required (as Crossman himself must have recognized in conceiving the idea for *The God That Failed*).

Not, however, any and all ex-Communists. Obviously Crossman and Koestler wanted, as they said, "ex-Communists capable of telling the truth about themselves," which for all practical purposes meant intellectuals who could also write. But here again there was an exclusionary principle at work, which becomes clear when we notice the absence of another category of ex-Communist intellectuals among whom could be found any number "capable of telling the truth about themselves" at least as well as the ones included in *The God That Failed*. This category was made up of those who had not only repudiated Communism as embodied in the Soviet Union, but who had also repudiated other variants of socialism and even Marxism itself as a philosophy. Some, like Max Eastman, became believers in and defenders of capitalism; others, like Whittaker Chambers, came to see belief in God as the ultimate defense against Communism. Neither of these types was represented in *The God That Failed*.

Instead, what Crossman and Koestler put together was a chorus of testimony against Communism from ex-Communists who had remained in some sense on the Left. It was a book which said, in effect, that one could be an anti-Communist without ceasing to be a liberal (in the American sense) or a socialist or even a Marxist—that, indeed, Communism was in reality the enemy of the true values of liberalism and Marxian socialism. To become an anti-Communist did not necessarily mean joining forces with the Right (which was thought by the Left to be as soft on fascism as the Left was suspected of being on Communism). But short of supporting fascism, opposition to Communism did not, according to Stephen Spender, even entail support for capitalism: "In writing this essay, I have always been aware that no criticism of the Communists removes the arguments against capitalism. The effect of these years of painful experiences has only been to reveal to me that both sides are forces producing oppression, injustice, destruction of liberties, enormous evils."

Now it must be said that *The God That Failed* would not in all likelihood have contributed so greatly to the legitimation of anti-Communism among writers and intellectuals if it had gone much further than it did. Certainly the examples of Eastman and Chambers, who had virtually no influence at all in the literary world of those days, suggests as much. At the same time, however, it must also be said that in refusing to recognize that capitalism was one of the indispensable constituent elements of Western democracy; that in itself it embodied a form of freedom and was on that account alone to be valued by all who valued freedom; and that, even as Spender was hurling his accusations, it was achieving a greater degree of widely shared prosperity throughout the Western world than anyone had ever dreamed possible of any economic system—the anti-Communism of these writers found no moorings in the real world and was cut loose to float in a utopian void. For if capitalism was, as Spender declared, as bad as Communism, where was one to turn?

In 1950, the answer seemed clear to most, or perhaps all, of the contributors to *The God That Failed* and to most, if not all, of their readers, myself emphatically included: some form of democratic socialism which would combine the virtues of the two systems and avoid the vices of both. Today, more than thirty years later, this answer seems to me to be based on some of the same illusions as the belief in Communism once was. The philosopher William Barrett has written of himself and other refugees from Marxism, who for a time found rest in the ideal of democratic socialism:

> How could we ever have believed that you could deprive human beings of the fundamental right to initiate and engage in their own economic activity without putting every other human right in jeopardy? And to pass from questions of rights to those of fact: everything we observe about the behavior of human beings in groups . . . should tell us that you cannot unite political and economic power in one center without opening the door to tyranny.

In other words, to reject Communism while trying to hold onto Marxism or socialism in some other form was—and is—intellectually insufficient. It left one in the position of blaming Stalin or Lenin or the special condition of Russia for the perversion or betrayal of the true heritage of Marxian socialism. In this way one remained free to go on believing in the utopian dreams of a transformed and redeemed world. Anyone under the sway of such utopian dreams was likely to evade the actual choices presented by reality in the here and now. However different the available alternatives might be as compared with each other, they were all bound to seem more or less equally undesirable by the standards of that "socialism" for whose full realization it was morally necessary to go on hoping and working.

On the one side, then, the rejection of Communism by itself could still leave one open to an endless repetition of the same political misjudgments that had been made in relation to the Soviet Union. To be sure, this was not generally the case with the authors of *The God That Failed* or most of the ex-Communists who had broken with the party by 1950. Their ideas might remain arrested in Marxism, but their firsthand experience of Communism protected them from

being led too far astray in taking the measure of other manifestations of the "god" that had failed them in its original
incarnation. This brand of anti-Communism turned out,
however, to be a much less effective antitoxin when absorbed by people who had not actually suffered from the
disease themselves—people, that is, who had never been
Communists or even loyal fellow travelers and who began
by accepting the disillusioned view of the Soviet Union with
which the ex-Communists ended.

For such people, the tradition represented by *The God
That Failed* was certainly enough, and more than enough,
to prevent the recurrence of illusions about the nature of
Soviet Communism. But it turned out to be inadequate as a
protection against comparable illusions, especially as applied
to what would later be called the Third World. Had socialism failed or been betrayed in the Soviet Union? No matter:
it would succeed in China; or if not there, in Cuba; or if
not there, in Chile; or if not there, in Vietnam; or if not
there, in Nicaragua. No failure, whatever its cost in human
misery, need discredit the dream. In every new instance, it
deserved the benefit of the doubt; a priori it had a superior
claim to the support of all humane and decent people than
the side against which it was fighting. Thus Susan Sontag,
whose "Kronstadt" finally came in 1982 after the imposi-
tion of martial law in Poland (though she was, in her own
words, "never a Communist and therefore not . . . a 'repen-
tant' ex-Communist of the god-who-failed variety"): "We
tried to distinguish *among* Communisms—for example,
treating 'Stalinism,' which we disavowed, as if it were an
aberration, and praising other regimes, outside of Europe,
which had and have essentially the same character."

Just as it was not enough intellectually to be anti-Communist, so it was not enough politically to be anti-Soviet. Since
the authors of *The God That Failed* took the Soviet Union

seriously, they knew (most of the time anyway) that expansionism was inherent in its very nature as a revolutionary Communist state. Since they took Communism seriously, they also knew that its spread to other countries was an evil to be resisted. Since, finally, the only power on earth that could effectively resist this evil was the United States, they had no choice but to support the new American determination to "contain" the Soviet empire within the boundaries set by the end of the Second World War. But this reliance on America to defend the world against the spreading tide of a system morally comparable to Nazism (against which the United States had also gone to war) still brought with it at most a grudging acknowledgment that the United States was the lesser of two evils. As Arthur Koestler once said in a different context: "The choice before us is merely that between a grey twilight and total darkness." And Stephen Spender, in *The God That Failed* itself, refused to concede even that much to the United States. "America, the greatest capitalist country," he wrote, "seems to offer no alternative to war, exploitation and destruction of the world's resources." This, at a time when America—*capitalist* America—was offering peace, freedom, and prosperity to formerly fascist countries like Germany, Italy, and Japan as well as to the war-torn and wounded democracies of Western Europe, which it had just expended blood and treasure to save from the totalitarianism of the Right, and which it was now prepared to spend blood and treasure to defend from the totalitarianism of the Left.

The neutralist attitude expressed in Spender's statement was the political face of the intellectual utopianism in which so many anti-Communists of the Left remained trapped. To be anti-Soviet while being simultaneously anti-American might ensure that the fastidious political sensibilities of a romantic poet like Spender would not be offended by a commitment to anything less than perfect. In the long run, however, such an attitude could not protect the world from the spread of Soviet power.

This should have been clear even in 1950, and it should have been clearer still in 1980 when the decline of American power in the post-Vietnam era had left Western Europe more exposed than ever to the continually growing threat of Soviet power. Yet the utopian fantasy of escape from the actual alternatives offered by reality in the here and now had by 1980 become more widespread, with the neutralist position foreshadowed by Spender in *The God That Failed* becoming prevalent throughout the European Left.

Moreover, at a time when hardly anyone, not even many Communists, still entertained the old illusions about the Soviet Union from which *The God That Failed* recorded an earlier retreat—the idea that the Soviet Union was a workers' paradise and the model for a better world—masses of people in the West, including many non-Communists, were being seduced by a new set of illusions about the Soviet Union. Now they were persuading themselves that the Soviet Union was devoted to peace and stability, and they were mouthing a new "line" of apologetics, according to which everything warlike and aggressive the Russians did on the international scene was a defensive response to bellicose American provocations.

It has become clear in retrospect, then (and poignantly so for me), that the kind of anti-Communism legitimized in *The God That Failed* was shot through with too many reservations and qualifications to stand firm against the pressures of the years ahead. Nevertheless, *The God That Failed* performed an enormous service for its time. It is therefore worth reading, and rereading, for its interest both as a classic historical document and as a cautionary object lesson. But it also demands to be read in its own right, for the light it continues to shed on the illusions about Communism that refuse to die in spite of one "Kronstadt" after another, and on the appeal those illusions continue to hold for so many writers and intellectuals who also remain as obdurately blind today to the values and virtues of democratic capitalism as Stephen Spender was in 1950.

2.

CAMUS AND HIS CRITICS

Are we in for a Camus revival? The indications are that we may be. Only three years after the appearance of Herbert R. Lottman's massive *Albert Camus: A Biography* (1979), we find ourselves presented with yet another biography, this one entitled simply *Camus,* by a British specialist in French literature named Patrick McCarthy who now teaches in the United States. Conor Cruise O'Brien, the influence of whose own critical monograph on Camus (published in 1970 under the title *Albert Camus of Europe and Africa*) is evident everywhere in McCarthy's book, has repaid the compliment by praising it as "the best comprehensive study of Camus in English." Yet while claiming to deal with "Camus's life, work, and times," McCarthy is so stingy with biographical detail and so niggardly in his account of the historical and cultural context in which Camus's life and work took shape that no one depending on him alone would be

able to make much sense of the story. For that Lottman is a
far better source. Like many biographers nowadays, he tells
us more than we perhaps need or want to know, but this is
on the whole preferable to not being told enough. On the
other hand, Lottman neither is nor pretends to be a literary
critic, whereas McCarthy is nothing if not critical. His real
purpose, in fact, is to determine "what remains of Camus"
as a writer. Here then is his judgment:

> Although he wrote a great deal, only a small part of his
> work remains alive. He was a bad philosopher and he has
> little to tell us about politics. His plays are wooden even if
> his novels are superb.

Quite apart from the question of whether this admirably
blunt statement is true, it represents an interesting turn in
Camus's reputation. When he was killed in an automobile
accident in 1960 at the age of forty-seven, Camus was still
widely regarded less as a great novelist than as a kind of
secular saint, the moral conscience of his generation. This is
not to say that his novels lacked for admiration and acclaim.
His first, *The Stranger,* published in 1942 when he was in
his late twenties, had been a great critical success (earning
the admiration of, among many others, Jean-Paul Sartre,
who would famously become first his close friend and then
his great antagonist). Five years later Camus's second novel,
The Plague, achieved not only critical acclaim but an enormous commercial success all over the world; and so too did
his third, and last, novel, *The Fall* (1956).

Yet when, a year after *The Fall* came out, Camus won
the Nobel Prize for literature, it was not taken either by him
or by anyone else as a tribute to his greatness as a novelist.
Nor would it have occurred either to him or to most of his
admirers that his stature rested entirely, or even largely, on
what was after all still a relatively slight body of fiction (to

be supplemented later only by a collection of stories entitled *Exile and the Kingdom*). However highly those three novels might have been esteemed, it was not in the least self-evident that they could by themselves bear the weight of the tribute paid to Camus in the Nobel citation—that he "illuminates the problems of the human conscience in our time." As though implicitly acknowledging this, Camus in his acceptance speech talked much more about the political duty of the writer—"to fight for freedom and to resist oppression"—than about cultural or aesthetic issues. "I cannot," he said, "live as a person without my art. And yet I have never set that art above everything else."

Neither did Camus's admirers. For them he was, to begin with, a great hero of the Resistance: the man who had edited the legendary underground newspaper *Combat* during the Nazi occupation of France. Indeed, *The Plague,* published in 1947, owed at least some of its great popularity to the fact that it was intended, and understood, as an allegory of the Resistance.

In addition to being a celebrated wartime hero, Camus was one of the most influential voices in the intellectual life of the postwar years. In what O'Brien calls "the loose literary and journalistic terminology of the period . . . in which existentialism meant finding life meaningless but finding reasons for carrying on all the same," Camus was bracketed with Sartre as an existentialist. Though he objected to this description of his philosophy, and though he may have been right on technical grounds to distinguish between Sartre's existentialism and his own "absurdist" perspective as developed in his long essay *The Myth of Sisyphus* (1942), the difference between the two was not easily apparent to the naked eye.

In any case, Camus the philosopher (or perhaps intellectual would be the better term) was valued by his contemporaries for the struggle he conducted against the nihilism of modern thought. "There is but one truly serious philosophical problem, and that is suicide": so runs the very first sentence of *The Myth of Sisyphus*. For if God is dead, as Nietzsche had proclaimed, and the universe has no meaning, why go on living? The "solution" to this problem, Camus says, is a "metaphysical revolt" against the religious illusions of divine purpose on the one side and despair at the absurd truth on the other. What is left after the death of God "is a destiny of which only the end is predetermined. Apart from this single predetermined fact of death, all, joy or happiness, is freedom. A world remains of which man is the sole master."

The effect this affirmation (which was echoed in novelistic terms in *The Stranger*) had on Camus's own contemporaries is summed up nicely by O'Brien:

> To a generation which saw no reason for hope it offered hope without reason. It offered a category—the absurd—in which logical, psychological, philosophical and even social and political difficulties could be encapsulated and it allowed the joy of being alive, in the presence of death, to emerge.

Finally, there was Camus the political thinker. Unlike his other roles as Resistance hero and as philosopher, his participation in the political debates of the postwar period brought Camus a great deal of animosity. On the two major issues that most concerned him—Algeria (where he was born into a working-class French family) and Communism (he had been a member of the Communist party for a few years in the thirties)—he took positions that were extremely unpopular in his own intellectual circle. On Algeria he was a reformist rather than a radical, specifically refusing to side with the terrorists of the FLN who were fighting for independence from France. "I have always denounced terrorism," he once said. "I must also denounce a terrorism which is exercised blindly, in the streets of Algiers for example, and which some day could strike my mother or my family. I believe in justice, but I shall defend my mother above justice."

This attitude certainly won Camus no friends in the cafés of St. Germain-des-Prés and other gathering places of the Parisian intelligentsia. But possibly because he had so clear a personal stake in the matter, his apostasy from the regnant orthodoxy on Algeria, if not exactly overlooked, did not lead to his excommunication from Parisian literary society.

His anti-Communism, by contrast, was unforgivable, as he discovered when *The Rebel* was published in 1951. In that book Camus developed a densely reasoned and historically grounded case against the actual political manifestations of the metaphysical nihilism he had dealt with in *The Myth of Sisyphus.* In arguing that the quest for a political solution to the absurdity or meaninglessness of the human condition invariably led to slavery and mass murder, Camus in *The Rebel* was of course attacking Communism as an ideology and its bloody practical consequences in the Soviet Union. For doing that, neither his previously unimpeachable credentials as a man of the Left nor his close personal friendship with Sartre could save him from assault in the pages of Sartre's own magazine, *Les Temps modernes,* first by a young critic named Francis Jeanson and then, in answer to a protesting letter from Camus, by Sartre himself. The controversy became world famous, and though most of Paris sided with Sartre, Camus had his supporters in other countries, especially the United States. Both *Partisan Review* and *Commentary,* for example, published accounts of the controversy which were sympathetic to Camus and harshly critical of Sartre's avowedly pro-Soviet position. Thus, while

Camus's political stance severely damaged his reputation at home, it undoubtedly added to his already growing stature in other countries as a man of conscience and a moral hero.

Like O'Brien before him, McCarthy is hostile to Camus's political writings and especially *The Rebel*. Its form, he says, is weak, it "distorts or neglects the thinkers [it] discusses," its language is "monotonously highflown," and even its one merit ("a long rhetorical lament on the religious conception of politics which flourished from the 30's to the 50's") amounts to nothing more than "an important banality." Clearly, however, it is the anti-Communism of *The Rebel,* rather than its intellectual or literary failings, that lies behind McCarthy's harsh critical judgment. Without entirely siding with Sartre (as O'Brien wholeheartedly does), he views Camus from the perspective for which, alas, no more graceful term than anti-anti-Communism has ever been found. From that perspective, he easily dismisses *The Rebel* as "yet another chapter in the 'God-that-failed' saga."

Given this bias against anti-Communism, McCarthy obviously cannot accept Camus as the "conscience" of his time. And indeed, he challenges the whole idea of Camus as a secular saint. "Retrospectively the tributes paid to him seem ridiculous. . . . He was not, for example, the Resistance warrior his admirers thought him," and he did not take the morally correct position on the Algerian war. The case for a revival of interest in Camus therefore comes back for McCarthy and those who share his perspective (O'Brien among them) to Camus the novelist.

The problem is that such a case is hard to make in strictly aesthetic or formalistic terms. In fact, it is virtually impossible even to talk about Camus's novels without reference to the philosophical and political issues with which he was above all else concerned. In saying this, I can point for confirmation to Camus's journals, where he explicitly spoke of each of his novels as one panel in a series of triptychs, with a play and a philosophical work comprising the other two. Thus *The Stranger* he coupled with *Caligula* and *The Myth of Sisyphus* under the rubric "Absurd"; the "Revolt" trilogy was made up of *The Plague, The Rebel,* and *The Just Assassins;* and *The Fall* was evidently to form part of yet another series on the theme of "Judgment."

In other words, Camus conceived of his imaginative works as dramatizations of the same ideas he was grappling with in his discursive writings. So much is this true of his plays that it robs them of any life of their own; and in any event, despite his lifelong obsession with the theater, Camus simply had no gift for it.

He did, however, have a considerable gift for fiction. In contrast to his plays, which are merely schematic illustrations of abstract ideas, his novels do take on a certain life of their own. They are lyrically evocative, they have enough narrative drive to carry the reader along, and they set off intriguing vibrations and resonances in the mind. Nevertheless, they are the novels of an intellectual, not the novels of a novelist, which is to say that they remain umbilically tied to the ideas whose creatures they so clearly are, never breaking free to establish themselves as autonomous works of art. Under the stringent control of an imperious intellect, these are tight little works, clenched and ungiving: even the longest and most leisurely of them, *The Plague,* yields no great abundance of character or incident or social detail. There are a few colorful portraits in *The Plague* and there are several dutiful sketches of the social milieu, but nothing approaching the anatomy of a city struck by a sudden calamity that Camus evidently intends to produce and that his material itself requires.

The Stranger and *The Fall* also offer highly colored characters who are nevertheless unrealized and unconvincing.

Meursault, the hero (or anti-hero) of *The Stranger,* is endowed with vivid external attributes, but is it really possible to believe in, let alone be engaged by, a character so affectless that he decides to marry a woman he scarcely knows or cares about because "It had no importance really," and who then shoots and kills a man because "one might fire, or not fire—and it would come to absolutely the same thing"?

Admittedly, a great many readers have been engaged and even fascinated by Meursault. But this is not, I would suggest, because he becomes real to them as (to take two very different murderers in fiction) Raskolnikov becomes real in *Crime and Punishment* or Clyde Griffiths in *An American Tragedy.* Raskolnikov is a Russian of a particular time and place whose ideas are a crucial element in his behavior; Meursault is a fictional contrivance whose behavior is a function of ideas in the mind of Camus. Clyde Griffiths is an American whose passions are so recognizable and so convincingly associated with the world in which he lives that the murder he eventually commits is believable both psychologically and sociologically: we accept it not only as a tragedy but as an *American* tragedy. If Meursault is believable at all, it is as a clinical psychopath, and if he carries any wider significance, it arises not from within the novel but almost entirely from the outside—in the idea that the psychopath is the representative modern man (a notion later espoused enthusiastically by Norman Mailer).

If the murder Meursault commits can only be understood with the help of ideas outside the novel itself, Jean-Baptiste Clamence, the narrator-hero of *The Fall,* is full of explanations of his own history. Yet, if anything, these explanations only serve to make that history less plausible. Why has Clamence thrown away a successful legal practice as a defender of widows and orphans, and a life full of comforts and prestige, to become a semicriminal hanging around a dock-

side bar in Amsterdam? Mainly, it seems, because in failing
to try to rescue a woman who had jumped off a bridge in
Paris one night, he had come face to face with his own hypocrisy as a great lover of justice. Now, even apart from the
fact that this incident has nothing to do with justice (it is
actually about courage), Clamence's response to it would
still remain a piece of hollow self-dramatization. Yet Camus
takes it seriously and clearly expects us to take it seriously.

If there is a critical case for these novels, then, it has to
rest on their standing as fables or allegories. Yet even as
such, they are less than fully satisfying. If we take *The
Stranger* at Camus's word as a fable of metaphysical rebellion against the absurd, we immediately run into a host of
problems. To begin with, it is hard to see in Meursault an
adequate expression of the defiant attitude he is presumably
supposed to represent. He is, of course, defiant in relation to
the consolations of religion, which he adamantly refuses, but
far from achieving freedom and mastery of the world, he
becomes a kind of automaton; far from finding happiness in
the simple pleasures of life, he enjoys nothing except swim-
ming; and far from resisting suicide, he, in effect, commits
it indirectly in the way he goes to his death.

The best that can be said for Meursault is that he exemplifies not a rebellion against nihilism but the condition itself.
Moreover, despite Camus's evident intention, he represents
not the moral consequences of nihilism that Dostoevsky
feared most of all ("If God is dead, everything is permitted"), but rather the spiritual effects stressed by Nietzsche when he said that with the death of God everything has
become *weightless*. Meursault kills, not because the prohibi-
tion against murder has, in effect, been lifted; he kills because murder, like everything else in life, has become incon-
sequential to him. He is as indifferent to the shedding of
blood as he is to the death of his mother or to the woman he

agrees to marry or finally to his own death. Such power as *The Stranger* possesses derives from the horror of this image of a life totally without meaning or affect. But Camus had other ideas and they were given their head to the detriment of what was most promising in his own material.

The Plague presents an even more interesting problem. O'Brien calls it "a great allegorical sermon" about the occupation of France and the Resistance, and McCarthy confirms that this is both what Camus intended and how the book was read when it first came out. But if we stop to ask what a city in the grip of plague has in common with a country occupied by an invading army, the answer would seem to be very little. The one is a natural calamity and, as such, morally and politically neutral; the other is a human phenomenon and is entirely moral and political in character. The significance of this point becomes immediately clear when we recall that whereas no one could possibly welcome or live happily with an outbreak of plague, a certain number of Frenchmen did welcome the Nazis, and a much larger number were quite content with the occupation. To put the point bluntly, while there can be no collaborators in a plague, there were plenty of collaborators with the Nazis.

This is also why it is conversely hard to accept Dr. Rieux and his band "as a group of resistants who are fighting against the overwhelming power of the Nazis" (McCarthy). To fight the Nazis took courage and even heroism, but since on the evidence of the novel itself "fighting" the plague evidently involved no greater danger of infection than remaining passive, Camus's attribution of courage to the doctor and his helpers seems puzzling.

But no more and no less puzzling, one might say, than the entire myth of the Resistance in general and of Camus's own role in particular—a myth to which *The Plague* made so notable a contribution. For as a number of recent books have been demonstrating to anyone still under the spell of this myth, the Resistance in France amounted to very little until a short time before the end of the war. Camus himself joined *Combat* only eight months before the liberation of Paris. Previously he had agreed to the elimination of a chapter on Kafka from *The Myth of Sisyphus* because a book celebrating a Jewish writer would not get by the German censors. But in doing this Camus did no more than most of the other intellectuals who were celebrated and celebrated themselves as heroes of the Resistance. Being anti-Nazi did not prevent Sartre, for example, from publishing books and putting on plays under the occupation—works that were not only passed by the Nazi censor but enthusiastically received by him. This did not make Sartre a collaborator, but it did not exactly make him a Resistance hero, either.

To be sure, Sartre was associated with the clandestine National Committee of Writers, but the only action of this committee mentioned by either McCarthy or Lottman (both of whom agree, incidentally, that it was dominated by the Communists) was the permission it gave Simone de Beauvoir to "accept the Goncourt Academy's prize if it were voted to her for her first novel. . . ." No doubt the committee did other things as well. Yet it is not easy to escape the impression that no great danger or heroism was involved in joining it.

As for Camus's clandestine activities in *Combat,* we get a good idea of what they entailed in the way of risk when Lottman follows an uncritically admiring account of them with the remark: "After the foregoing, it will be more difficult than ever to persuade the reader that during the same period in which Camus was helping to publish the underground edition of *Combat* . . . he was also making his debut as a playwright in the Paris theater."

With this background in mind, it becomes easier to

understand why Camus could only write about the Nazi occupation and the Resistance in allegorical terms. Confronting it directly in a realistic mode would have required facing up to the element of (shall we say?) the absurd—the word applies here with cruel accuracy—in the idea that the French, and especially the French intellectuals, acted nobly and bravely during the occupation. A few, of course, did; a few writers even refused to publish under the German occupation, regarding it as a form of collaboration to submit to Nazi censorship. But only a relative handful of Frenchmen joined the Resistance until the point when an Allied victory seemed assured, and most anti-Nazi writers persuaded themselves that publishing under the occupation was a form of resistance rather than of collaboration. They may well have been right. But heroic they most certainly were not.

In treating the entire episode allegorically, Camus was able to take refuge from such issues in the posturing rhetoric that is for many of us the least attractive feature of the French intellectual style. But in translating the occupation into an outbreak of plague, and thereby inevitably making nonsense of the idea of heroic resistance, was Camus half-consciously struggling to tell himself, and the world, the truth?

I think he was, and I also suspect that *The Fall* should be read as part of the same struggle to achieve honesty (which is, after all, the only true heroism of a writer as a writer). Clamence has been interpreted by some critics as a satirical portrait of "Sartre and other progressive intellectuals," which would make *The Fall* an attack on the hypocrisy of their professed concern for the poor and the oppressed. I agree with O'Brien and McCarthy in rejecting this view, but I do not agree with them in seeing *The Fall* as a reflection of Camus's feelings about Algeria. Since *The Fall* is the only one of Camus's novels not set in Algeria, this interpretation forces O'Brien into the tortured argument that the very absence of Algeria from the book makes it "painfully present." Yet Clamence lives in the Jewish Quarter of Amsterdam, which he himself calls "the site of one of the greatest crimes in history." Consequently, it seems more plausible to associate *The Fall* not, as O'Brien in his obsession with the problem of colonialism would wish, with Algeria, but with the issues raised by *The Plague*. Clamence's confessions of cowardice and hypocrisy, that is, may perhaps be taken as the expression of a higher stage in his creator's progress toward a more truthful account of the behavior of French intellectuals under the Nazis than as a reflection of Camus's supposedly troubled conscience over Algeria.

I say supposedly, because of all the issues that engaged Camus, the one on which he had least reason to accuse himself of cowardice and hypocrisy was Algeria. He was morally courageous in holding out against the enormous pressures on him to support the FLN, and he was intellectually courageous in telling the truth about his reasons. When he declared that he chose his mother above justice, he was, as O'Brien puts it, choosing "his own tribe" against an abstract ideal of universal justice. A greater heresy against the dogmas of the Left is hard to imagine, and in committing it he may have earned the reproaches of his literary friends, but he did nothing to earn his own.

In denying that *The Fall* is about Algeria, I do not mean to argue that it is mainly about the myth of the Resistance. What is it about then? The title, the name of the hero, and many details scattered throughout suggest that Camus is talking about religion rather than politics. O'Brien says *The Fall* is "profoundly Christian . . . above all in its pervasive message that it is only through the full recognition of our sinful nature that we can hope for grace." Camus himself endorsed this interpretation when O'Brien offered it in a review of the novel at the time of its publication. But one can only say that if this was Camus's intention, the novel he actually wrote failed to realize it. For it is impossible to make coherent sense of *The Fall* as a Christian allegory. Clamence has nothing in common with John the Baptist except his name, and his fall has nothing in common with the biblical Fall. Unintegrated into the narrative, the Christian imagery becomes merely arbitrary; it is a means of pretending to a level of significance and profundity that the novel itself as a novel—or even as a fable—does nothing to earn.

My own view is that *The Fall* does indeed reflect Camus's great debate with Sartre, but that in the figure of Clamence, Camus is primarily attacking himself rather than Sartre "and other progressive intellectuals." Certainly there are many similarities between Clamence and his creator. As the herald of the great new age of freedom and justice he had envisaged in his *Combat* editorials, Camus could easily be seen as a kind of John the Baptist, and like Clamence he had prospered mightily (in reputation and with women) in this role. But like Clamence too he eventually discovered that he lacked the courage to risk everything in the fight for freedom and against the forces of slavery, and as a punishment for remaining "neutral in the quarrel between God and Satan" he was now condemning himself to a life in limbo as a "judge-penitent."

But is it true that Camus saw the struggle between the Western democracies and the Soviet Union as equivalent to "the quarrel between God and Satan"? And did he really see himself as neutral? That he regarded Communism as satanic is clear from *The Rebel,* but it is equally clear that he did not regard the bourgeois democracies as godlike. Like so many intellectuals then, and now, he could give wholehearted support only to some alternative possibility which did not yet exist. He was, that is, a utopian. Yet, unlike many intellectuals then, and now, Camus also understood that utopianism was the main spiritual source of the murderous totalitarianism embodied in the Soviet Union and therefore the modern secular equivalent of satanism. As Sartre and Jeanson rightly charged, the logic of this analysis led directly to a pro-American position, and in trying to escape that logic Camus was presuming to speak as (in Jeanson's words) "the High Priest of Absolute Morality." A choice had to be made within the historical realm; Sartre, for his part, and despite regrets and misgivings, chose the Soviet Union and was not afraid to say so; Camus, in effect, chose the United States and *was* afraid to say so.

What I am suggesting is that Camus believed in his heart that this attack on him was valid, and that the cowardice and hypocrisy of which he accuses himself in *The Fall* are the cowardice and hypocrisy involved in his failure to side as clearly with the democracies as Sartre was siding with the Communists—and all for fear of being dismissed as a man of the "Right" and thereby losing his standing as a secular saint. "If, finally, truth seemed to me on the Right," Camus defiantly declared, "I would be there." Yet the truths of *The Rebel* were on the whole the truths of the "Right," as that term was understood by all concerned in this debate, and Camus was *not* there. Indeed, when Jeanson taunted him with the fact that "right-wing" reviewers had praised *The Rebel*, Camus, instead of asserting that in this case that was where truth was, justified himself by pointing to the criticisms made of him by the Right, and he counterattacked by hurling the dread epithet "bourgeois" at Jeanson (an accusation Sartre promptly hurled back at him).

It was, I would guess, because of all this shying away from commitment that Camus castigated himself as neutral; and this it was too that made him a "penitent." But he also remained a "judge," and while castigating himself he continued to condemn Sartre (of whom he was surely thinking when he wrote the passage in which Clamence ridicules the "atheistic novelist" whose "satanism is virtuous").

Although this interpretation makes, I believe, more sense than any other, no more than any other does it establish *The Fall* as a work of art autonomously dramatizing and enacting its own meanings. As the allegorical detail in *The Plague* serves to obscure the truth about the occupation, so the Christian symbolism here both obfuscates Clamence's confession and provides Camus with a pretentious way to avoid the full and rigorous accounting with himself he so desperately needed and wanted to undertake.

Writing at the height of the radical fevers of the late sixties and in "horror at the sight of the moral capital of *La Peste* [The Plague] being drawn on in support of the values of the cold war," O'Brien nevertheless praised Camus the artist who, he claimed, "both flinched from the realities of his position . . . and also explored with increasing subtlety and honesty the nature and consequences of his flinching." In other words, Camus's novels indicate that if he had lived he would have given up on anti-Communism and moved to the Left.

Today, as Patrick McCarthy tells us disapprovingly, Camus is being extolled in France by a new generation "as the man who resisted Communist pressure during the cold war and who attacked the Russian concentration camps in language that Solzhenitsyn would repeat," while Sartre is denounced "as too Marxist, too pro-Communist and too dogmatic." Once again, then, it has become necessary to deprive the anti-Communist cause of Camus, and once again his novels— puffed up and misread—are brought in to do the job. But whereas in 1970 O'Brien interpreted the novels as the record of Camus's growing disillusion with the political values of *The Rebel,* McCarthy (who also dismisses *The Rebel* as

Camus's "worst book") reads the novels as an escape into the loftier realms of art from those "dreary, angry controversies" with Sartre and others that poor Camus had to "put up with."

The truth is almost exactly the opposite of this. With all his faults, and with all its faults, the best of Camus is in *The Rebel*. His novels, moreover, are the record not of a growing disillusion with, or transcendence of, the convictions expressed in that book, or in the controversy with Sartre, but of an unsuccessful struggle to summon up the full courage of those convictions. If, then, there is to be a Camus revival in the United States, the Camus who should be revived is the one to whom justice is finally being done in France: the Camus of *The Rebel,* not the travesty urged upon us first by O'Brien and now by McCarthy in the name of art but in the actual service of their anti-anti-Communist political passions.

3.

IF ORWELL WERE ALIVE TODAY

"Dickens," George Orwell once remarked, "is one of those writers who are well worth stealing," which was why so many different groups were eager to claim him as one of their own. Did Orwell foresee that someday he too would become just such a writer? Almost certainly he did not. In 1939, when he wrote those words about Dickens, he was still a relatively obscure figure, and, among those who knew his work at all, a highly controversial one. Only a year earlier, his book about the Spanish Civil War, *Homage to Catalonia,* had been rejected on political grounds by his own publishers in both Britain and the United States; and far from being claimed by contending factions as one of their own, he was closer to being excommunicated and excoriated by them all. Nevertheless, by the time of his death in 1950 at the age of forty-six, he had become so famous that his very name entered the language and has remained there in the form of the adjective "Orwellian."

At first, this great status rested almost entirely on the tremendous success, both critical and commercial, of his two last novels, *Animal Farm* (1945) and *Nineteen Eighty-Four* (1949). Thanks to them, all his other books, including several early novels that were scarcely noticed at the time of their publication, as well as literary essays, book reviews, and even fugitive pieces of dated journalism, came back into print and are still easily available. As these earlier works became better known, they gradually enhanced Orwell's posthumous reputation. For example, the much maligned *Homage to Catalonia* was pronounced "one of the important documents of our time" by Lionel Trilling when it was finally published in the United States after Orwell's death. And when in 1968 *The Collected Essays, Journalism and Letters of George Orwell* came out in four massive volumes, the occasion was seized upon by another American critic, Irving Howe, to proclaim Orwell not only "the best English essayist since Hazlitt, perhaps since Dr. Johnson," but also "the greatest moral force in English letters during the last several decades." Bernard Crick, one of Orwell's most recent British biographers, goes, if possible, even further, placing him with Thomas Hobbes and Jonathan Swift as one of the three greatest political writers in the history of English literature (greater, in other words, than even Edmund Burke and John Stuart Mill).

This enormous reputation by itself would make Orwell "one of those writers who are well worth stealing." It is, after all, no small thing to have the greatest political writer of the age on one's side: it gives confidence, authority, and weight to one's own political views. Accordingly, a dispute has broken out over what Orwell's position actually was in his own lifetime, and what it might have been if he had survived to go on participating in the political debates that have raged since the day of his death.

Normally, to speculate on what a dead man might have said about events he never lived to see is a frivolous enterprise. There is no way of knowing whether and to what extent he would have changed his views in response to a changing world; and this is especially the case with a writer like Orwell, who underwent several major political transformations. On the other hand, the main issues that concerned Orwell throughout his career are still alive today, often in different form but often also in almost exactly the same form they took when he wrote about them. This is why so many of his apparently dated journalistic pieces remain relevant. Even though the particular circumstances with which they deal have long since been forgotten, the questions they raise are questions we are still asking today and still trying to answer.

If this is true of much of Orwell's fugitive journalism, it becomes even more strikingly evident when we consider some of his major works: *Animal Farm* and *Nineteen Eighty-Four* among his novels, and, among his discursive writings, *Down and Out in Paris and London* (1933), *The Road to Wigan Pier* (1937), and *Homage to Catalonia* (1938), not to mention many of the wonderful essays collected in *Inside the Whale* (1940), *Dickens, Dali and Others* (1946), and *Shooting an Elephant* (1950). So relevant do all these works seem today that to read through them is to be astonished, and a little depressed, at the degree to which we are still haunted by the ghosts of political wars past.

When Orwell wrote his essay on Dickens, the two main groups trying to "steal" Dickens were the Marxists and the Catholics. (That they could automatically be taken as equivalent to Left and Right is one interesting measure of how things have changed in the past forty years.) The two main groups contending over Orwell today are the socialists on the one side and, on the other, the disillusioned former socialists who have come to be known as neoconservatives. The socialists, of whom Crick is a leading representative, declare that Orwell was a "revolutionary" whose values can only be (as Crick puts it) "wilfully misunderstood . . . when he is claimed for the camp of the cold war." For their part, the neoconservatives deny that Orwell was a revolutionary; they think of him instead as a major critic of revolutionism. And they do indeed claim him for "the camp of the cold war" in the sense that they see in his work one of the great prophetic warnings against the threat of Soviet totalitarianism. Thus the Committee for the Free World, an organization made up mainly of neoconservative intellectuals (and with which I am associated), publishes material under the imprint "Orwell Press" and in general regards Orwell as one of its guiding spirits.

As a writer, Orwell is most admired, and rightly so, for the simplicity and straightforwardness of his style. "Good prose," he said, "is like a window pane." He valued such prose for its own sake, on aesthetic grounds, but he also believed that in political discourse clarity was a protection against deceit: "In our time, political speech and writings are largely the defense of the indefensible. . . . Thus political language has to consist largely of euphemism, question-begging and sheer cloudy vagueness." Since Orwell wrote about politics in a language that not only avoided those vices but succeeded marvelously in the art of calling things by their proper names and confronting questions with plainness and precision, one might think that nothing would be easier than defining his point of view. The problem is, however, that he wrote so much and changed his mind so often— mostly on small issues but also on large ones—that plausible evidence can be found in his work for each of the two contending interpretations of where he stood.

As a very young man, Orwell was, by his own account,

a "Tory anarchist." But at the age of thirty or thereabouts he converted to socialism and kept calling himself a socialist until the day he died. Crick therefore has no trouble in piling up quotations that support the socialist claim to possession of Orwell. He does, however, have a great deal of trouble in trying to explain away the side of Orwell that has given so much aid and comfort to antisocialists of all kinds. For, avowed socialist though he certainly was, Orwell was also a relentless critic of his fellow socialists from beginning to end.

Thus no sooner did he declare his allegiance to socialism than he began taking it upon himself to explain why so many decent people were put off by his new political faith. "One sometimes gets the impression," he wrote in *The Road to Wigan Pier,* "that the mere words 'Socialism' and 'Communism' draw towards them with magnetic force every fruit-juice drinker, nudist, sandal-wearer, sex-maniac, Quaker, 'Nature Cure' quack, pacifist and feminist in England." Shortly after delivering himself of this observation, and while he still regarded the Communists as comrades in the struggle for socialism, he went to fight against Franco in the Spanish Civil War. There he learned two things: that the Spanish Communists were more interested in furthering the aims of Soviet foreign policy than in making a socialist revolution at home, and that the left-wing press in England (and everywhere else) was full of lies about what was actually going on in Spain. For the next few years, much of his writing was devoted to attacks on the Stalinists and their fellow travelers, who, in those days of the "Popular Front," included almost everyone on the Left.

These attacks were written from what can loosely be described as a Trotskyist or revolutionary-socialist perspective based on, among other things, the proposition that England was hardly, if at all, better than Nazi Germany. But with

the outbreak of World War II, a new Orwell was born—
Orwell the English patriot. "My Country, Right or Left," he
now declared in one of his most memorable phrases, and
went on to excoriate the "anti-British" attitudes that had
been so fashionable on the Left throughout the 1930s and to
which he himself had temporarily subscribed.

Then, toward the end of the war, and with the defeat of
fascist totalitarianism in sight, Orwell began brooding more
and more on the possibility that Communist totalitarianism
might turn out to be the inevitable wave of the future. In
Animal Farm, written while the Soviet Union was still a
wartime ally of the Western democracies, he produced a
satire on the Russian Revolution so unsparing that it could
be and usually was interpreted as a repudiation of all hopes
for a benevolent socialist revolution. Like *Homage to Catalonia* before it, the manuscript was rejected as too anti-Soviet
by the first few publishers to whom it was submitted. One
of the publishers in this case was no less a personage than
T. S. Eliot, whose own aggressive conservatism did not prevent him from doubting that Orwell's was "the right point
of view from which to criticize the political situation at the
present time."

Finally there was *Nineteen Eighty-Four,* which came out
just at the height of the cold war and very shortly before
Orwell's death. In that novel, Orwell portrayed the England
of the future as a totalitarian society ruled over by a Commu-
nistlike party in the name of "Ingsoc" ("newspeak" for English socialism). He later explicitly denied that in using this
term he had intended to cast any aspersions on the British
Labour party, of which he was a (highly critical) supporter,
let alone that he was attacking socialism itself. Nevertheless,
neither in *Animal Farm* nor in *Nineteen Eighty-Four* was
there any trace of the idea that a socialist revolution could
be accomplished without a betrayal of the ideals of liberty

and equality to whose full realization socialism was in theory committed.

No wonder Crick has so much trouble staking the socialist claim to Orwell. No wonder too that other socialists of varying stripe like Isaac Deutscher and Raymond Williams have said that Orwell was not really one of them.

If Orwell was a great political writer—and I think he was, though I would not place him quite so high as Crick does— it is not because he was always right in his strictly political judgments. The plain truth is that he was more often wrong than right. For example, he predicted that the British Conservatives (the "Blimpocracy") would never go to war against Hitler; then, when they did, he refused to believe, and he doubted "whether many people under fifty believe[d] it either," that England could "win the war without passing through revolution."

In addition to making many mistaken political predictions, he was also capable of serious errors of political valuation, as when he joined briefly in the fashionable cry of the mid-1930s to the effect that there was no difference between fascism and liberalism. And even after correcting errors of this kind, he was capable of backsliding into such similar absurdities as saying that British rule in India was as bad as Hitler's rule in Europe, or that British policy toward Greece in 1945 was no different from "the Russian coercion of Poland."

Wrong though he so often was about particular events, however, Orwell in every stage of his political development was almost always right about one thing: the character and quality of the left-wing literary intellectuals among whom he lived and to whom he addressed himself as a political writer. More than anything else, the ethos of the left-wing literary intelligentsia was his true subject and the one that elicited his most brilliant work. Indeed, whatever ideas were

fashionable on the Left at any given moment were precisely
the ones he had the greatest compulsion to criticize. And
the fact that he criticized them from within only added authority to the things he said—so much so that I wonder
whether this was why he insisted on clinging so tenaciously
to his identity as a man of the Left.

It is largely because of Orwell's relation to the left-wing
intelligentsia that I believe he would have been a neoconservative if he were alive today. I would even suggest that he
was a forerunner of neoconservatism in having been one of
the first in a long line of originally left-wing intellectuals
who have come to discover more saving political and moral
wisdom in the instincts and mores of "ordinary" people than
in the ideas and attitudes of the intelligentsia. "One has to
belong to the intelligentsia to believe things like that," he
wrote in 1945 after listing several egregious examples relat-
ing to the progress of World War II; "no ordinary man
could be such a fool." This remark has become especially
well known in recent years, but it is only one of many passages of similar import scattered throughout Orwell's writings.

Nor was it only on political issues that Orwell defended
the "ordinary man" against the left-wing intelligentsia. Even
in the mid-1930s, during his most radical period, he attacked
Cyril Connolly's novel *The Rock Pool* for suggesting that
"so-called artists who spend on sodomy what they have
gained by sponging" were superior to "the polite and sheep-
like Englishman." This, he said, "only amounts to a distaste
for normal life and common decency," and he concluded by
declaring: "The fact to which we have got to cling, as to a
lifebelt, is that it *is* possible to be a normal decent person
and yet to be fully alive."

This streak of populism, always strong in Orwell, became
even more pronounced with the outbreak of World War II,

when it took the form of a celebration of England and the English character. As a corollary to becoming a whole-hearted patriot—and in coming to see patriotism as a great and positive force—Orwell lashed out more ferociously than ever at the British intelligentsia:

> . . . the really important fact about so many of the English intelligentsia [is] their severance from the common culture of the country. . . . England is perhaps the only great country whose intellectuals are ashamed of their own nationality. In left-wing circles it is always felt that there is something slightly disgraceful in being an Englishman and that it is a duty to snigger at every English institution. . . . All through the critical years many left-wingers were chipping away at English morale, trying to spread an outlook that was sometimes squashily pacifist, sometimes violently pro-Russian, but always anti-British. . . . If the English people suffered for several years a real weakening of morale, so that the Fascist nations judged that they were "decadent" and that it was safe to plunge into war, the intellectual sabotage from the Left was partly responsible.

Is it any wonder that the neoconservatives see Orwell as a guiding spirit when everything he says here has been echoed by them in talking about the American intellectuals of today? And when Orwell was charged with "intellectual-hunting" by a leading young pacifist named Alex Comfort (who, as though to confirm Orwell's diagnosis of the phenomenon of which Comfort was a typical specimen, would go on to greater heights of fame in later years as the author of *The Joy of Sex*), he replied in terms that have been echoed in similar arguments by the neoconservatives as well: "It is just because I do take the function of the intelligentsia seriously that I don't like the sneers, libels, parrot phrases and financially profitable back-scratching which flourish in our English literary world. . . ."

Another and related reason for thinking that Orwell would be a neoconservative if he were alive today lies in his attitude toward pacifism. For a very brief period in his youth Orwell flirted with pacifism, but nothing could have been more alien to his temperament and he soon broke off the affair. By 1938 he was writing (and in language that shows how far he was willing to go in speaking plainly, even when euphemism might better have served his own political position):

> If someone drops a bomb on your mother, go and drop two bombs on his mother. The only apparent alternatives are to smash dwelling houses to powder, blow out human entrails and burn holes in children with lumps of thermite, or be enslaved by people who are more ready to do these things than you are yourself; as yet no one has suggested a practical way out.

And again in 1940, when a British defeat seemed likely: "There is nothing for it but to die fighting, but one must above all die *fighting* and have the satisfaction of killing somebody else first."

Moved by such feelings, Orwell came to write about pacifism with an even fiercer edge of scorn and outrage than before. Later he would regret using the term "objectively pro-Fascist," but that is what he now accused the pacifists— or "Fascifists," as he called them—of being (for, "If you hamper the war effort of one side you automatically help that of the other"); he also attacked them for "intellectual cowardice" in refusing to admit that this was the inescapable logical implication of their position; and he said that they were hypocritical "for crying 'Peace!' behind a screen of guns." But in trying to imagine where Orwell would have stood if he were alive today, the key sentence in his attack on pacifism is this: "Insofar as it takes effect at all, pacifist pro-

paganda can only be effective *against* those countries where
a certain amount of freedom of speech is still permitted; in
other words it is helpful to totalitarianism."

Everything I have just quoted was written at a time when
Nazi Germany was the main totalitarian enemy. But here is
what Orwell said about pacifism at the very moment when
the defeat of Hitler was imminent and when the Soviet
Union was about to replace Nazi Germany as the most powerful embodiment of totalitarianism in the world:

> Pacifist propaganda usually boils down to saying that one
> side is as bad as the other, but if one looks closely at the
> writings of the younger intellectual pacifists, one finds that
> they do not by any means express impartial disapproval but
> are directed almost entirely against Britain and the United
> States. Moreover they do not as a rule condemn violence as
> such, but only violence used in defense of the Western
> countries. The Russians, unlike the British, are not blamed
> for defending themselves by warlike means. . . .

The "real though unadmitted motive" behind such propa-
ganda, Orwell concluded, was "hatred of Western democracy and admiration for totalitarianism."

It is hard to believe that the man who wrote those words
in 1945 would have felt any sympathy for the various "objectively" pacifist antidefense movements of today, about which
the very same words could be used without altering a single
detail. I can even easily imagine that Orwell would have
been still angrier, if he had lived, to see so many ideas that
have been discredited, both by arguments like his own and
by historical experience, once again achieving widespread
acceptability. It goes without saying that he would have opposed the unilateral disarmament that became the official
policy of the British Labour party under the leadership of
his old journalistic colleague Michael Foot. He understood,

after all, that "Despotic governments can stand 'moral force' till the cows come home; what they fear is physical force." But I think he would also have opposed such measures as the nuclear freeze and a unilateral Western pledge of no-first-use of nuclear weapons. Given the conception of totalitarianism he developed in *Animal Farm* and *Nineteen Eighty-Four* as a totally closed system in which lies become truth at the dictate of the party, the notion that a verifiable disarmament agreement could be negotiated with the Soviet Union would surely have struck him as yet another pacifist "illusion due to security, too much money and a simple ignorance of the way in which things actually happen."

As for no-first-use, Orwell surely would have seen this as a form of unilateral disarmament by the West (since it would make Soviet superiority in conventional military power decisive on the European front), as well as a euphemistic screen behind which the United States could withdraw from its commitment to the defense of Western Europe under the hypocritical pretext of reducing the risk of nuclear war.

Nor is it likely that Orwell would have been reconverted to pacifism by the fear of nuclear weapons. As a matter of fact, he thought that "the worst possibility of all" was that "the fear inspired by the atomic bomb and other weapons yet to come will be so great that everyone will refrain from using them." Such an indefinite Soviet-American stalemate, he predicted, would lead to precisely the nightmare he was later to envisage in *Nineteen Eighty-Four* ("the division of the world among two or three vast totalitarian empires unable to conquer one another and unable to be overthrown by an internal rebellion").

This does not mean that Orwell contemplated the possibility of a nuclear war with equanimity, or that he did not on other occasions say that it could mean the destruction of civilization. Nevertheless, in 1947, the very year in which the cold war officially began, Orwell wrote: "I don't, God knows, want a war to break out, but if one were compelled to choose between Russia and America—and I suppose that is the choice one might have to make—I would always choose America." Later that same year, he made the point again: "It will not do to give the usual quibbling answer, 'I refuse to choose.' . . . We are no longer strong enough to stand alone, and . . . we shall be obliged, in the long run, to subordinate our policy to that of one Great Power or another."

The same essay contains another one of those uncanny passages we so often come upon in Orwell that could be applied to our situation today without altering a single detail:

> To be anti-American nowadays is to shout with the mob. Of course it is only a minor mob, but it is a vocal one. . . . I do not believe the mass of the people in this country are anti-American politically, and certainly they are not so culturally. But politico-literary intellectuals are not usually frightened of mass opinion. What they are frightened of is the prevailing opinion within their own group. At any given moment there is always an orthodoxy, a parrot-cry which must be repeated, and in the more active section of the Left the orthodoxy of the moment is anti-Americanism. I believe part of the reason . . . is the idea that if we can cut our links with the United States we might succeed in staying neutral in the case of Russia and America going to war. How anyone can believe this, after looking at the map and remembering what happened to neutrals in the last war, I do not know.

So much for Orwell's attitude toward the neutralism that lies at the basis of what in Western Europe is called the "peace movement" today.

To understand the force and the courage of Orwell's forthright repudiation of the idea that there was no significant moral difference between the United States and the Soviet Union, we need only remind ourselves from the example of *The God That Failed* that neither anti-Americanism nor neutralism was confined exclusively to the pro-Soviet Left. When Orwell said, "I particularly hate that trick of sucking up to the Left cliques by perpetually attacking America while relying on America to feed and protect us," he could easily have been referring to his friend Stephen Spender's remarks in *The God That Failed* that America "seems to offer no alternative to war, exploitation and destruction of the world's resources" and that, no less than the Soviet Union, the United States was a "force producing aggression, injustice, destruction of liberties, enormous evils." In any event, so far as Orwell was concerned, the people in the British Labour party who openly wanted "to appease Russia" were more honest: they at least understood "that the only big political questions in the world today are: for Russia–against Russia, for America–against America, for democracy–against democracy."

Despite Crick's sophistical protestations, then, there can be no doubt that Orwell did belong in "the camp of the cold war" while he was still alive. Nor can there be much doubt that, if he were alive today, he would have felt a greater kinship with the neoconservatives who are calling for resistance to Soviet imperialism than with either the socialist supporters of détente or the coalition of neutralists and pacifists who dominate the "peace movement" in Europe and their neo-isolationist allies in the United States.

For consider: Orwell's ruling passion was the fear and hatred of totalitarianism. Unlike so many on the Left today, who angrily deny that there is any difference between totalitarianism and authoritarianism, he was among the first to insist on the distinction. Totalitarianism, he said, was a new and higher stage in the history of despotism and tyranny—a system in which every area of life, not merely (as in authoritarian regimes) the political sphere, was subjected to the control of the state. Only in Nazi Germany and the Soviet Union had totalitarianism thus far established itself, and of the two the Soviet variety clearly seemed to Orwell to be the more dangerous.

Indeed, Orwell's loathing for Nazi Germany was mild by comparison with his feeling about the Soviet Union. He was sufficiently serious in his opposition to fascism to risk his life in struggling against it in Spain (where as a soldier he was very nearly killed by a bullet through the neck). Yet he showed surprisingly little awareness of how evil Nazism actually was. Not only did he never write anything like *Animal Farm* about the Nazi regime; there is scarcely a mention in all his writings of the death camps. (Two of his closest friends, Arthur Koestler and T. R. Fyvel, saw a relation between this curious "blind spot" about Nazism and his equally curious hostility to Zionism.)

When Orwell wrote about the dangers of totalitarianism, then, whether in his essays or in *Nineteen Eighty-Four,* it was mainly the Communist version he had in mind. To be sure, he followed no party line, not even his own, and he could always be relied on to contradict himself when the impulse seized him. At one moment he would denounce any move to establish good relations with the Russians, and at another moment he might insist on the necessity of such relations.

But these were transient political judgments of the kind that, as he himself ruefully acknowledged, were never his strongest suit. What he most cared about was resisting the spread of Soviet-style totalitarianism. Consequently, he "used a lot of ink" and did himself "a lot of harm by attacking the successive literary cliques" that had denied or tried to play down the brutal truth about the Soviet Union, to appease it, or otherwise to undermine the Western will to resist the spread of its power and influence.

If he were alive today, he would find the very ideas and attitudes against which he so fearlessly argued more influential than ever in left-wing centers of opinion (and not in them alone): that the freedoms of the West are relatively unimportant as compared with other values; that war is the greatest of all evils; that nothing is worth fighting or dying for; and that the Soviet Union is basically defensive and peaceful. It is impossible to imagine that he would have joined in parroting the latest expressions of this orthodoxy if he had lived to see it return in even fuller and more dangerous force.

I have no hesitation, therefore, in claiming Orwell for the neoconservative perspective on the East-West conflict. But I am a good deal more diffident in making the same claim on the issue of socialism. Like Orwell, most neoconservatives began their political lives as socialists; and most of them even followed the same course Orwell himself did from revolutionary to democratic socialism. Moreover, those neoconservatives who were old enough to be politically active in 1950, the year Orwell died, would still at that point have joined with him in calling themselves democratic socialists. About thirty years later, however, most of them had come around to the view expressed by William Barrett in explaining why he had finally given up on his long and tenaciously held faith in "democratic socialism" (the telling quotation marks are Barrett's). I have already quoted from Barrett's explanation once,* but it is worth quoting again:

* See above, p. 28.

How could we ever have believed that you could deprive human beings of the fundamental right to initiate and engage in their own economic activity without putting every other human right in jeopardy? And to pass from questions of rights to those of fact: everything we observe about the behavior of human beings in groups, everything we know about that behavior from history, should tell us that you cannot unite political and economic power in one center without opening the door to tyranny.

The question is: would Orwell, in the light of what has happened in the three decades since his death, have arrived eventually at a position similar to Barrett's? Crick is certain that he would not—that he would have remained a socialist, and a militant one. I am not so sure.

Orwell was never much of a Marxist and (beyond a generalized faith in "planning") he never showed much interest in the practical arrangements involved in the building of socialism. He was a socialist because he hated the class system and the great discrepancies of wealth that went with it. Yet he also feared that the establishment of socialism would mean the destruction of liberty. In an amazingly sympathetic review of F. A. Hayek's *The Road to Serfdom,* Orwell acknowledged that there was "a great deal of truth" in Hayek's thesis that "socialism inevitably leads to despotism," and that the collectivism entailed by socialism brings with it "concentration camps, leader worship, and war." The trouble is that capitalism, which "leads to dole queues, the scramble for markets, and war," is probably doomed. (It is indeed largely as a result of the failure of capitalism that the totalitarian world of *Nineteen Eighty-Four* comes into being.)

Suppose, however, that Orwell had lived to see this prediction about capitalism refuted by the success of the capitalist countries in creating enough wealth to provide the vast

majority of their citizens not merely with the decent mini-
mum of food and housing that Orwell believed only socialism could deliver, but with a wide range of what to his
rather Spartan tastes would have seemed unnecessary luxu-
ries. Suppose further that he had lived to see all this accomplished—and with the year 1984 already in sight!—while
"the freedom of the intellect," for whose future under socialism he increasingly trembled, was if anything being
expanded. And suppose, on the other side, he had lived to
see the wreckage through planning and centralization of one
socialist economy after another, so that not even at the sacrifice of liberty could economic security be assured.

Suppose, in short, that he had lived to see the aims of what
he meant by socialism realized to a very great extent under
capitalism, and without either the concentration camps or
the economic miseries that have been the invariable com-
panions of socialism in practice. Would he still have gone
on mouthing socialist pieties and shouting with the anti-
capitalist mob?

Perhaps. Nothing has been more difficult for intellectuals
in this century than giving up on socialism, and it is possible
that even Orwell, who so prided himself on his "power of
facing unpleasant facts," would have been unwilling or unable to face what to most literary intellectuals is the most
unpleasant fact of all: that the values of both liberty and
equality fare better under capitalism than under socialism.

And yet I find it hard to believe that Orwell would have
allowed an orthodoxy to blind him on this question, any-
more than he allowed other "smelly little orthodoxies" to
blind him to the truth about the particular issues involved in
the struggle between totalitarianism and democracy: Spain,
World War II, and Communism.

In Orwell's time, it was the left-wing intelligentsia that

made it so difficult for these truths to prevail. And so it is too with the particular issues generated by the struggle between totalitarianism and democracy in our own time, which is why I am convinced that if Orwell were alive today, he would be taking his stand with the neoconservatives and against the Left.

PART TWO

The Adversary Culture

4.

F. R. LEAVIS: A REVALUATION

From the point of view of historical piety it seems deplorable that so little notice should have been taken of the fiftieth anniversary of the birth of *Scrutiny,* the English critical journal that exerted so great an influence on the entire Anglo-American literary world from 1932 until its demise about two decades later. Yet there was a certain justice contained in this impiety. For important though *Scrutiny* undoubtedly was in its day, anyone interested in how and why it really mattered can more profitably spend his time on the work of its editor and chief contributor, F. R. Leavis, than by reading through the back issues. It is true that many people besides Leavis himself wrote for *Scrutiny* and that a few of the *Scrutiny* regulars—D. W. Harding, L. C. Knights, Marius Bewley, and Q. D. Leavis—were excellent critics in their own right. But it is equally true that they—not to mention their less distinguished fellows—rarely dissented in any significant degree from Leavis's ideas and judgments. *Scrutiny*, in short, *was* Leavis. How could it have been otherwise? So powerful was his influence that no one who ever came near him could escape it; and so dogmatic was he that anyone who disagreed with him about anything was soon banished from the pages of the magazine. Leavis liked to say of his critical judgments that they had been arrived at "not dogmatically but deliberately." In fact, he used this phrase, taken from Dr. Johnson's *Preface to Shakespeare,* as the epigraph to one of his most important books, *The Great Tradition.* But there is something even more comical in Leavis's disclaimer of dogmatism than in Johnson's, particularly in connection with *The Great Tradition,* with its unforgettably audacious first sentence: "The great English novelists are Jane Austen, George Eliot, Henry James and Joseph Conrad—to stop for the moment at that comparatively safe point in history."

Another thing Leavis liked to say about critical judgment was that it takes the form of the question " 'This is so, isn't it?' the question asking for confirmation that the thing is *so,* but prepared for an answer in the form, 'Yes, but—,' the 'but' standing for corrections, refinements, precisions, amplifications." Yet having studied with Leavis at Cambridge for three years in the early fifties, I can testify at firsthand that nothing could have been farther from the spirit of his own procedure than such an open and easy give-and-take of tentative opinions ready to be revised. And having once again read through nearly all his published writings (including the half-dozen or so books he produced after the demise of *Scrutiny,* which he outlived by twenty-five years), I can hardly imagine anyone other than a sycophantic disciple failing to smile, or even to laugh out loud, at the idea that Leavis ever offered his judgments in the form of a question. The first sentence of *The Great Tradition* is entirely characteristic of Leavis's critical pronouncements, and whatever else it may be, it is not a question. As for being "prepared for an answer in the form, 'Yes, but—,' " there are many samples scattered throughout his writings of how he responded to disagreement, and at least ninety-nine percent of them are accompanied by scorn, anger, abuse, and righteous claims of misrepresentation.

An especially vivid case involves Leavis's 1962 reply to C. P. Snow's argument (in his famous little book *The Two Cultures and the Scientific Revolution*) that the attitudes of the literary world had for more than a century been infused by a "Luddite" hostility to industrial civilization. Entering the controversy, which had by then become worldwide, Lionel Trilling sided with Leavis on the substantive issue but chided him for the cruelty of his attack on Snow. Whereupon Leavis shot back: "I have to comment that, in thus lending himself to the general cry that I have 'attacked' Snow . . . Mr. Trilling, who passes as a vindicator of the critical function, seems to me guilty of *la trahison des clercs.*" So much for "Yes, but—."

The same ferocity comes out in Leavis's response to Sir Herbert Grierson's disagreement with his negative view of Milton: "What is there to say, then, except that the scholar who commits himself to such pronouncements, distinguished authority on seventeenth-century matters as he certainly is, has no claim to be treated as a critical authority on the verse of the period—or any verse." This of the man whose great anthology of metaphysical poetry, published in 1921, had provided the occasion for an essay by T. S. Eliot (actually a review of the anthology) which changed the course of English literary history and incidentally exercised a lifelong influence on Leavis himself.

As a teacher Leavis tried to be gentler when crossed, but it still required courage, or foolhardiness, to venture a dis-

agreement with him. To express the view, say, that Wordsworth's Immortality Ode was a great poem (not, after all, a
self-evidently outlandish opinion) would elicit from Leavis a
look of such long-suffering, such pain, such weary and hope-
less resignation that one might have refrained from speaking
up out of compassion for him, even if one were not already
terrorized into silence by the fear of convicting oneself of
an incapacity for "independent critical judgment" (a quality
Leavis actually believed he was helping his students to
develop).

In thus poking fun at what was certainly a major failure
of self-knowledge in Leavis, my intention is not to denigrate
his work as a literary critic. A failure of self-knowledge is always (as Leavis himself demonstrated over and over again)
a radical fault in a poet or a novelist, but it need not be
seriously disabling in a critic. At any rate, unlike Leavis himself, I do not believe that his dogmatism was something to
be ashamed of and denied. On the contrary, to me it seems
one of his most valuable qualities and the essential ground
of his greatness as a critic.

For in spite of everything that can be said against him,
Leavis *was* a great critic. He was great, first of all, in his
gifts of sensibility and intellect. Here again, I can testify
from firsthand experience. Although as judged by his own
criteria he was a very bad teacher, it was nevertheless an
overwhelming experience to sit in one of his tiny classes (or
"supervisions," as they are called at Cambridge) and listen
to him day after day analyze poems or passages of English
prose, explaining in the most concrete terms why these lines
could only have been written in 1710 or why that stanza
was superior to this and what extraliterary implications
might be drawn from the difference. Not only did he seem
to have read all the books there were to be read, but he had

read them all—including the ones he despised—with a full-ness of attention and an alertness of perception to which his students unhappily recognized they could attain only at rare moments in their own reading. Beyond this he seemed to know everything there was to know about the historical context of the poems and novels he discussed. And finally, all this digested and mastered knowledge, awesome in its sheer quantity, was in the living service of a powerful mind and a seriousness about literature the like of which was hard to match even in the early fifties, when seriousness about literature was taken for granted in universities on both sides of the Atlantic.

To get some idea of what Leavis was like at these supervisions, a good place to go is to the section entitled "Judgement and Analysis" in one of his last books, *The Living Principle* (1975), where—comparing a series of poems by Wordsworth, Hardy, Lawrence, Eliot, and others—he treats us to a dazzling demonstration of what used to be called "practical criticism." But of course the same qualities that were so vividly present at his supervisions are abundantly evident throughout his writings. In fact, there was a much smaller gap between Leavis on paper and Leavis in the flesh than was the case with such other major contemporary critics as Lionel Trilling or Edmund Wilson.

Which brings up the much-vexed question of Leavis's prose style. Leavis has often been accused of writing badly, and it cannot be denied that his sentences tend toward the crabbed and thorny. As with Henry James's celebrated convolutions, this habit, always present in his prose, grew worse with age, so that by the time we get to his late works we regularly come upon passages like this: "The dangerousness of Andreski lies in his assuming that his discursive common-sense use of language *is* the use of language for thought—is,

76

THE BLOODY CROSSROADS

in the distinctive spirit that limits it, essentially, and more
or less co-terminously, that; and inducing or conforming in
most of his readers the blankness he reveals."

Thus Leavis at his worst. At his best, however, and for
much of the time (even occasionally in the books of his old
age), Leavis writes in a style that combines the spontaneity
and flexibility of the spoken voice (*his* voice) with the sharp-
ness and precision of careful composition. Summing up a
long discussion of the relation between imagery and the
emphasis on sound, as opposed to sense, in *Paradise Lost,* he
once observed: ". . . Milton's preoccupation with 'music'
precludes any strength in the kinds of imagery that depend
on what may be called a realizing use of the body and action
of the English language. . . ." This formulation is perhaps
ungainly and its own "music" is harsh. But it certainly uses
"the body and action of the English language" and in its
own way exemplifies the virtue whose absence from Milton's
verse it deplores. That is, instead of inducing "a generally
relaxed state of mind" in us, which "brings nothing to any
arresting force, but gives us a feeling of exalted significance,
of energetic effortlessness, and of a buoyant ease of command," Leavis's charged, pointed, and evocative characterizations work to slow us down, to compel our careful attention,
to make us think about what we are feeling.

This is why he has to be read very carefully, or not at all.
Nor is there much point in reading his books (with the possible exception of *The Great Tradition* and a few essays here
and there) unless one is prepared to consult the texts with
which they deal. Leavis is addressing an "educated public"
familiar with the poems and novels he writes about, not a
casual lay audience. But what his prose thereby loses in ac-
cessibility, it gains in immediacy and allusive richness.

Leavis was great, then, in his gifts. But he was also great
in what he achieved with those gifts. As a self-proclaimed

disciple of T. S. Eliot, he undertook a systematic development of the "hints" (a favorite word of his) thrown out by
Eliot's early critical essays and embodied concretely in Eliot's
poetic practice. This involved a "revaluation" of the entire
history of English literature in the light of the revolution
effected by Eliot's poetry. "Sensibility alters from generation
to generation in everybody, whether we will or no, but expression is only altered by a man of genius," Eliot had written, and Leavis (though he developed more and more reservations about Eliot as the years wore on) never deviated
from the belief that Eliot *was* that man of genius for the
generation of which they were both members. But Eliot had
also said that such an alteration of expression must necessarily alter the way the present looks at the past. As a critic,
Eliot himself had already sketched the outlines of the new
shape of the past, most notably in elevating Donne and the
other metaphysical poets of the seventeenth century above
Milton and in downgrading the nineteenth-century Roman-
tics (especially Shelley). With the additional help of such
Eliotic concepts as the "dissociation of sensibility" and the
"objective correlative," Leavis set out to fill in the details of
this outline. But before he got very far he found himself
running into conflict with Eliot both on specific judgments
and in his general perspective, so that the new map he eventually drew of English literature, while owing its original
inspiration to Eliot, turned out to be very much his own
(and in many respects antithetical to Eliot's ideas).

This new map was largely charted in a series of three
books: *New Bearings in English Poetry* (1932), which
started with the late Victorians and ended with the early
modernists (Yeats, Pound, and Eliot); *Revaluation* (1936),
which flashed back to the seventeenth century and carried
the account forward to the point where *New Bearings* had
begun; and *The Great Tradition* (1948), which covered the

English novel from the eighteenth century to the early twentieth. Having thus fixed the basic canon, Leavis later modi-
fied and added to it with two books on D. H. Lawrence
(*D. H. Lawrence: Novelist* [1955] and *Thought, Words,
and Creativity* [1976]) and *Dickens the Novelist* (written in
collaboration with his wife, Q. D. Leavis, and published in
1970). Most of the pieces collected in *The Common Pursuit*
(1952) and *Anna Karenina and Other Essays* (1955) are also
best read and can in any case only be fully understood if
they are seen as extended footnotes or appendices that en-
large or refine, or in some instances revise, the judgments
according to which the place of a given writer in this canonical tradition is determined.

"Critics have found me narrow," Leavis once said, and
then went on to complain of misrepresentation (as this most
critical of all critics always did whenever he himself was
criticized). Yet narrow he most assuredly was, and as with
the related charge of dogmatism, he would have been more
honest if he had confessed to it and then claimed it as a
virtue. For Leavis's narrowness was by no means the symp-
tom of ignorance or of a limited ability to appreciate. It was,
rather, inseparable from a willingness to commit himself
clearly and without protective coloration to the critical judgments and the discriminations he was bent on establishing.
The purpose these judgments and discriminations served was
not primarily aesthetic (a word he hated). Leavis's aim, in
fact, was almost the opposite of the spirit expressed in the
famous concluding chapter of *The Renaissance,* in which
Walter Pater speaks of cultivating the ability to discern
"some tone on the hills or the sea . . . choicer than the rest."
What, by contrast, Leavis was trying to do through the exercise of discrimination was "to ascertain the master-current
in the literature of an epoch, and to distinguish this from all
minor currents." These words come not from Leavis himself

but from a critic no one accuses of narrowness, Matthew Arnold, who moreover called such an effort "the critic's highest function."

Working back, then, from his own "epoch," Leavis traced "the map or chart of English poetry as a whole" (his words this time) running from Shakespeare through Ben Jonson, Donne, Pope, Blake, Wordsworth, Keats, Hopkins, and finally T. S. Eliot. By the time we get to the nineteenth century in this account, however, and in spite of Wordsworth, Keats, and Hopkins, the master-current moves out of poetry and into the novel, whose greatest practitioners (the ones discussed in *The Great Tradition*) are—and Leavis says so explicitly—the true successors to Shakespeare. Indeed, Dickens—at first excluded from the line of great novelists because, although "a great genius . . . the genius was that of a great entertainer [who] had for the most part no profounder responsibility as a creative artist than this description suggests"*—later becomes for Leavis the "second Shakespeare."

Then, in the twentieth century, as the master-current of verse flows into T. S. Eliot, so the great novelistic tradition culminates in D. H. Lawrence, after which both lines dry up, leaving a literary landscape littered with the corpses of talented writers cut off for lack of proper nourishment, if not for lack of praise and influence. Commenting in this connection on W. H. Auden, the most celebrated poet in the generation that followed Eliot, Leavis is at his most scathing:

> Mr. Auden's honesty there is no need to question; it may perhaps be said to manifest itself in the openness with which his poetry admits that it doesn't know how serious it supposes itself to be. . . . But it was not clear-sightedness that made him an irresistible influence. The "political aware-

---

* The qualification refers to *Hard Times,* to which a special section of *The Great Tradition* is devoted.

ness" and the "personal guilt" into which he "shamed a generation" were of a kind that it cost them very little to be shamed into. They asked for nothing better, and his poetry stilled any uncomfortable suspicion that there might be something better (if less comforting) to ask for. There it was, flatteringly modern and sophisticated, offering an intellectual and psychological profundity that didn't challenge them to any painful effort or discipline, and assuring them that in wearing a modish Leftishness they could hold up their heads in a guaranteed rightness. . . .

Leavis is speaking here of Auden's poetry of the thirties, but the later Auden, who cast off the "modish Leftishness" of his youth and embraced religion, fares no better with Leavis. Indeed, the whole point for Leavis is that Auden's "remarkable talent" remained permanently arrested "at the stage of undergraduate 'brilliance.' "

As for the novelists who followed Lawrence, Leavis's attitude toward them all was summed up, give or take a detail or two, in what he said about C. P. Snow:

. . . as a novelist he doesn't exist; he doesn't begin to exist. He can't be said to know what a novel is . . . he can't do any of the things the power to do which makes a novelist. He tells you what you are to take him as doing, but he can give you no more than the telling. . . . It is not merely that Snow can't make his characters live for us—that he lacks *that* creative power; the characters as he thinks of them are so impoverished in the interests they are supposed to have and to represent that even if they had been made to live, one would have asked of them, individually and in the lump: "What of life is there here, and what significance capable of engaging an educated mind *could* be conveyed through such representatives of humanity?"

In explaining why, on the one hand, a brilliant young poet like Auden should have failed to mature properly and, on the other, why an untalented novelist like Snow should have acquired so great a reputation, the answer in Leavis's scheme of things is simple: Bloomsbury. In Leavis's lexicon Bloomsbury stands for much more than the group of writers around Lytton Strachey, Virginia Woolf, Clive Bell, and the rest. It stands for "metropolitan literary society and the associated University milieux"—which is to say, weeklies like the *Observer* and the *Times Literary Supplement,* literary magazines like Cyril Connolly's *Horizon,* the BBC, and the English faculties of Oxford and Cambridge. This was the "establishment" against which Leavis stood in permanent rebellion (he even called himself an "outlaw"), and it was the prevalence of its "currency values" and the monopolistic power of its ideas and standards that accounted for Auden's failure to "become acquainted with serious criticism and the standards of maturity," first at the university and then when he entered "the larger literary world." And it was this same milieu, controlled by the same cliques and coteries, that some twenty years later pronounced Snow a major novelist and a great sage.

Although Leavis could speak very respectfully of a Bloomsbury writer like E. M. Forster, he nevertheless saw in the original circle, and still more in the literary world that grew out of it, a set of qualities that made serious criticism impossible: "Articulateness and unreality cultivated together; callowness disguised from itself in articulateness; conceit casing itself safely in a confirmed sense of high sophistication; the uncertainty as to whether one is serious or not taking itself for ironic poise: who has not at some time observed the process?"

The values associated with these qualities were even worse. Taking issue with a prominent Bloomsbury don's patronizing description of George Eliot as a Puritan who "admired truthfulness and chastity and industry and self-restraint,

[and] disapproved of loose living and recklessness and deceit and self-indulgence," Leavis writes:

> I had better confess that I differ (apparently) from Lord David Cecil in sharing these beliefs, admirations, and disapprovals, so that the reader knows my bias at once. And they seem to me favorable to the production of great literature. I will add (exposing myself completely) that the enlightenment or aestheticism or sophistication that feels an amused superiority to them leads, in my view, to triviality and boredom, and that out of triviality comes evil.

But harsh as Leavis was toward any contemporary writer who won the approval of "Bloomsbury" (the very fact of being acclaimed by such a "system" was sufficiently damning by itself), he could be almost as harsh toward its favored writers of the past; and whenever its enthusiasms happened to coincide with his, he would be driven to demonstrate that the writer in question was being valued for all the wrong reasons. With this in view (and seeing Leavis's war with Bloomsbury as a continuation of the Roundhead-Cavalier split in English culture), Lionel Trilling once suggested that the reason Leavis was so rough on Congreve and Meredith was not that he really considered them so bad but rather that Bloomsbury considered them so good.

There was undoubtedly a certain truth in Trilling's speculation. But important as this factor may have been in the ferocity with which Leavis's negative judgments were expressed, it is also important to recognize that there was nothing gratuitous or arbitrary about those judgments themselves. The point was invariably to illuminate the positive alternatives and to keep them clearly and sharply in view. For if there was a master-current in poetry running from Shakespeare all the way to Eliot, there was another line running from Spenser through Milton, Dryden, Shelley, and Tennyson that represented not so much a minor current as a flow in the wrong direction. In the one tradition, the distinctive genius of English found its fullest realization by rooting itself in the spoken language and therefore also in the life being lived around it. In the other tradition there was a tendency to use Latin or Italian as a model; and with this linguistic habit went a correlative disposition to think of poetry as removed from ordinary life (the life expressed, precisely, in the spoken language) and as belonging to a "higher" realm or a world of dreams, cut off not only from daily life but from the concerns of an engaged and critical adult mind.

In the novel, too, of course, the "great tradition" was made up of writers with "a vital capacity for experience" and "a kind of reverent openness before life." But in the greatest novelists there was more to be found than the "creation of real characters . . . external abundance, and . . . a loosely generous provision of incident and scene." In the likes of Jane Austen, George Eliot, Henry James, and Joseph Conrad there was all this, but it was informed, controlled, and organized by "a marked moral intensity."

Neither in George Eliot nor in any other great novelist did such moral intensity manifest itself in didacticism; it was embodied and dramatized—or, as Leavis puts the point, "it justifies itself as art in the realized concreteness that speaks for itself and *enacts* its moral significance." Nor in the greatest novelists could a Flaubertian preoccupation with form be separated (as in Leavis's view it was in Flaubert himself) from "imaginative sympathy, moral discrimination and judgment of relative value." Thus Conrad, whose obsession with form sent him to school to the works of Flaubert, was the greater novelist "because of the greater range and depth of his interest in humanity and the greater intensity of his moral preoccupation."

Leavis's own moral intensity comes into play even when he writes about poetry. Perhaps the most striking example in all his writings, and the one that is most likely to startle a "sophisticated" reader today, is the essay on Shelley in *Revaluation*. There, after demonstrating through quotation and analysis that Shelley's poetry "offers the emotion in itself, unattached, in the void" in contrast to Wordsworth, in whose work the emotion always "seems to derive from what is presented" (Leavis leans heavily here, as so often he does, on Eliot's concept of the "objective correlative"), he remarks: "But criticism of Shelley has something more important to deal with than mere bad poetry; or, rather, there are badnesses inviting the criticism that involves moral judgment." He then goes on to show through an examination of several of Shelley's best-known works how "the wrong approach to emotion, the approach from the wrong side or end (so to speak)" leads to "viciousness and corruption" in the form of a self-regarding pathos, a luxurious self-pity, and a perverse "love of loathing."

Whether or not one finds such an analysis valid or persuasive—and I emphatically do—and whether or not one accepts Leavis's judgments in every particular—and I just as emphatically do not*—one should be able to recognize that the new "map or chart" he drew of English literature represented a great intellectual achievement. Leavis said of Dr. Johnson (with whom he has often and rightly been compared) that he spoke with perfect authority for the Augustan tradition of taste in which he was educated; one can say of Leavis that he spoke with perfect authority for the

---

* For what it may be worth, I think that among the novelists, Leavis overrates Conrad and Lawrence and underrates Fielding and Trollope; among the poets, I would say he does less than justice to Yeats, Byron, and Dryden, that he is too hard on Auden and too easy on Pound. Moreover, he has little of value to say, for good or ill, about any writer who has come along since the 1930s.

twentieth-century revolution in taste out of which his sensibility emerged.

For it was Leavis more than anyone else, certainly more than T. S. Eliot, the father of the revolution, who explored its implications. He did so, moreover, with the utmost critical rigor, by which I mean an unfailing responsibility not only to the relevant textual evidence but also to the requirements of consistency and coherence. Taste taken seriously has a logic of its own, and to this logic Leavis was relentlessly true. Here, and not in any arbitrary principle of exclusion, was the real source of his "narrowness." To think that Thackeray, say, was a truly great novelist was to commit oneself to certain standards and valuations that stood in the way of properly appreciating George Eliot or Henry James. Conversely, to understand how the genius of Keats developed into mature greatness was to become aware of why and how Shelley's genius failed to do so and why and how Tennyson represented a falling off. From the absence of such awarenesses as these came "the misdirection and waste of much talent" in writers like Auden and the wanton squandering by the present of the precious spiritual resources of the past.

But Leavis's narrowness flows from a deeper source as well. He is always called a Puritan, and so he was in his moral standards and even more markedly in his moral seriousness. But if we remind ourselves of the intimate connection between puritanism and the Old Testament, we begin to see that what Leavis, the descendant of Huguenots, was trying to do in drawing a new map of English literature was the secular equivalent of what the rabbis of old did in fixing the scriptural canon. Some of the many reputedly sacred books of ancient Israel, they decided, had actually been written under divine inspiration and therefore belonged in the Bible; others were holy but not divinely inspired and were placed among the apocryphal writings; still others were condemned as heretical. So with Leavis, for whom literature was surely a substitute for the Bible on which the puritanism of his Protestant ancestors had been nourished, and for whom literary criticism accordingly became a substitute for devotional meditation and scriptural exegesis. (The presence of this element perhaps explains why Leavis's critical writings are so much more charged than the superficially similar but "secular" exegetical analyses produced by such American "New Critics" as Cleanth Brooks, Robert Penn Warren, and Allen Tate, with whom he was once imprecisely associated. It also explains why Leavis was once accused, more precisely, of believing that "literary criticism will save us.")

Leavis was, then, a great literary critic—great in his gifts and great in his achievement. But, to use one of his own favorite phrases, "discriminations are called for," and in his case they are called for by a set of amazingly simplistic ideas about contemporary civilization, ideas that C. P. Snow was right in characterizing as "Luddite." As Leavis denied that he was dogmatic or narrow, so he also denied that he was a Luddite. Yet reading through his works—from such early tracts as *Culture and Environment* (written in 1930 in collaboration with Denys Thompson) and *Education and the University* (1943) to the essays of his last years collected in *Lectures in America* (1969) and *Nor Shall My Sword* (1972)—one finds all the standard clichés about the malign effects of industrialism. Nor, on the other side, is there a good word anywhere in these writings for the improved standard of living brought about by the advance of technology; the very phrase "standard of living" is used only to deride the crass materialism of the people he called "technologico-Benthamites."

So blinded was Leavis by these clichés that even in the sixties and seventies, a time when the educated classes of the entire Western world were seized by a frenzy of hatred for technology and all its works, he imagined that contemporary culture was dominated by a Benthamite worship of technology; he even thought the student uprisings of the late sixties (which he also scorned) were an outgrowth of the same ethos, whereas of course the youth culture of that period was as antagonistic to the ideal of material and technological progress as Leavis himself. In a hideously ironic sense, those young people of the counterculture were more *his* students than C. P. Snow's. In failing to see this, Leavis was guilty of another failure of self-knowledge.

Unlike his dogmatism and his narrowness, which contributed to his strength and his achievement as a literary critic, however, Leavis's Luddism had a damaging effect on his critical judgment. We see this most clearly in his wild misrepresentation of D. H. Lawrence. To Leavis, Lawrence was the greatest writer of our age, much greater than T. S. Eliot, his only serious rival; as such he elicited from Leavis an attitude so reverential that the prose of *D. H. Lawrence: Novelist* sometimes sounds more like prayer than criticism.

To be sure, Leavis, so famous for his harshness, was equally vehement in his enthusiasms; when he spoke of great literature he was invariably transported into a state resembling rapture. In the classroom, quoting a passage he admired, his face would take on an obviously devotional aspect: the eyes closed, the brow furrowed, and the head subtly inclined upward toward the heavens. On paper the same attitude took the form of an uninhibited outpouring of superlatives. For example, on Henry James:

It is a measure of our sense of the greatness of Henry James's genius that discussion should tend to stress mainly what he failed to do with it. But what achievement in the art of fiction—fiction as a completely serious art addressed to the adult mind—can we point to in English as surpassing his?

Or on Conrad:

But he was not only by far the greatest of the Edwardians; there is more to be said than that . . . Conrad is among the very greatest novelists in the language—or any language.

On George Eliot (and Tolstoy):

George Eliot, of course, is not as transcendently great as Tolstoy, but she *is* great, and great in the same way. The extraordinary reality of *Anna Karenina* (his supreme masterpiece, I think) comes of an intense moral interest in human nature that provides the light and courage for a profound psychological analysis. . . . Of George Eliot it can in turn be said that her best work has a Tolstoyan depth and reality.

Finally, on Dickens:

Our purpose is to enforce as unanswerably as possible the conviction that Dickens was one of the greatest of creative writers; that with the intelligence inherent in creative genius, he developed a fully conscious devotion to his art, becoming as a popular and fecund, but yet profound, serious and wonderfully resourceful practising novelist, a master of it. . . .

Reverential though such passages are, however, when we read Leavis on any writer other than Lawrence, and whether we agree or disagree with him, we recognize, in the sure precision of his descriptions and in the illuminating characterizations of the work before him, the presence of a disinterested critical mind trying, in line with Matthew Arnold's prescription, "to see the object as in itself it really is." But we recognize no such thing in reading him on Lawrence. It is not that he is uncritical in the sense of accepting everything Lawrence ever wrote with equal enthusiasm. With the significant exception of a passage devoted to the ugliness of industrial England, he finds *Lady Chatterley's Lover* offensive, and he even takes issue with Lawrence's own high estimate of *The Plumed Serpent* as "my most important thing so far." But the tone in which he expresses his negative judgment of these books sounds oddly apologetic, especially set beside the firm decisive voice we hear when he diagnoses the weaknesses of such other canonical writers as James and Conrad.

Conversely, in discussing the novels he considers Lawrence's greatest, *The Rainbow* and *Women in Love,* Leavis becomes uncritical in the strict sense of taking intention for realization, conception for execution, assertion for dramatic enactment. Commenting, for example, on a passage in *The Rainbow* in which Lawrence puts his own thoughts into the mind of one of his characters, Leavis writes: "This, of course, is Lawrence himself—our awareness of that is overriding, without our being disabled from accepting it as Anna." Yet the whole point is that we *are* "disabled from accepting it as Anna," just as we are disabled from accepting any other character in these novels by Lawrence's overbearing refusal or inability to let them be. There is no life in them because they are nothing but counters in the polemical play of his ideas.

That Leavis should elevate these novels, which violate in the most fundamental way his own most important criteria, to a supreme position bespeaks an astonishing disorientation. It can, I believe, be traced to the same sin Lawrence himself commits in *The Rainbow* and *Women in Love* (though not in some of his shorter works). As Lawrence bullies his characters here entirely into the service of his own Luddite ideas about the contemporary world, so Leavis uses Lawrence in the service of the same ideas; and as Lawrence thereby sins against the impersonality without which the novelistic art is perverted into preaching, so Leavis sins against the disinterestedness in whose absence literary criticism becomes a species of covert ideologizing.

Only a few years after *D. H. Lawrence: Novelist* was published, the values for which Leavis so preeminently stood as a critic were subjected on both sides of the Atlantic to an assault of unprecedented force—and not from the "technologico-Benthamites" on whom his polemical guns were rigidly trained. Leavis in his obsessive way repeatedly cited the remark of a scientist he met sometime during the late sixties or early seventies who told him that computers could write poems. Obviously, the reason he seized on this remark is that it seemed so perfect a crystallization of the "spiritual philistinism" bred by the technologico-Benthamite culture. What Leavis never understood, however, was that the naive and ignorant attitude toward literature, and things of the spirit generally, expressed in the scientist's remark was harmless as compared with the attack on literature that was even then being mounted from within the literary culture itself. Thus, for example, the classical scholar Norman O. Brown, whose book on Freud, *Life Against Death,* had made him into one of the major gurus of the counterculture, later said:

> We are in bondage to authority outside ourselves: most obviously . . . in bondage to the authority of books. . . . This bondage to books compels us not to see with our own eyes;

compels us to see with the eyes of the dead, with dead eyes. . . . There is a hex on us, the specters in books, the authority of the past; and to exorcise those ghosts is the great work of magical self-liberation.

Several prominent literary critics, while not going quite as far as Brown, made their own contribution to the denigration of literature. Marshall McLuhan declared without notable regret that literature was obsolete and was being replaced by television; Richard Poirier wrote about the Beatles in terms that might have seemed excessive if applied to Shakespeare; Susan Sontag celebrated another singing group, the Supremes; and Leslie Fiedler stopped writing about literature altogether and devoted himself to the study of comic books. Evidently the slogan "against interpretation," which Sontag used as the title of her first collection of essays, applied only to literature and not to popular culture, even at its lowest levels.

Though these developments achieved their most virulent form in America, they had their counterparts in England, too. Yet so obsessed was Leavis with "technologico-Benthamism" that he never even noticed them. If he had noticed them there is no doubt that he would have found them utterly repugnant, even evil. How could he not, given his fundamentally religious belief in the centrality of literature and of the need for an intelligent critical community? But if he had noticed, would he have recognized the influence of D. H. Lawrence (and also of his equally beloved Blake) in the spread of these anti-intellectual attitudes within the literary world? Would he have recognized in the counterculture the traces of some of his own most stubbornly held and persistently reiterated attitudes toward industrial society and all its works? Is it because these recognitions might have forced themselves into his consciousness if he had seen what was really going on around him in the last years of his life that he so resolutely refused to look?

Whatever the answers to such questions, it would of course be the height of absurdity to place too heavy an emphasis on this aspect of Leavis. Even granting that he himself was to some extent implicated in this poisonous assault on everything he held most dear, the antidote is nevertheless to be found in his own writings, with their incomparable case for the importance of literature and the wonderful demonstration they provide of a great critical mind at work.

As such, these writings have a special importance for us just now: a time when the spiritual resources of the literary past either lie buried in their library vaults or are mined by a new monopoly of "deconstructionist" critics for whom literary works have no "determinate" meaning and therefore no independent existence. Either way, the squandering and misuse of these indispensable and irreplaceable treasures have become far more wanton than even Leavis, with all his desperate forebodings, could have imagined possible.

As for criticism of contemporary writing, the situation just now in America is commensurately worse than it was in the England of Leavis's prime. Such once vital American centers of serious criticism as *Partisan Review* and *Kenyon Review* have long since given up, leaving the field almost entirely to our own local variant of Bloomsbury, headquartered in *The New York Review of Books* and the *New York Times Book Review* and devoted to the making and breaking of literary reputations in accordance with cliquish "currency-values" far more debased than the original Bloomsbury's ever were.

Because he so vividly embodies an alternative conception of the function of criticism—and despite his indiscriminately negative attitude toward new writing—Leavis's own words about George Eliot, that "for us in these days . . . she is a peculiarly fortifying and wholesome author, and a suggestive one," apply for us in *these* days with equal force to him.

5.

HENRY ADAMS: THE "POWERLESS" INTELLECTUAL IN AMERICA

In 1917, about a year before he died, Henry Adams remarked in a letter to one of his oldest friends: "I once wrote some books myself, but no one has even mentioned the fact to me for more than a generation. I have a vague recollection that once some young person *did* mention an anecdote to me that came from one of my books and that he attributed it to some one else." A good deal of what is most characteristic of Adams is contained in these two valedictory sentences written at the age of seventy-nine. They are haughty; they are drenched in bitterness; and they ignore any and all realities that might spoil the dramatic effect at which they aim. The reader of these sentences would never suspect, for example, that only four years earlier a privately printed book by Adams, which he had finally allowed a commercial publisher to issue after an endless courtship, had broken all the firm's records for advance sales. Nor would anyone suspect that two years later, in 1915, the same firm would try once again to get the rights to yet another of his privately printed books (which, said the editor, aroused in him "more publishing covetousness" than any book he had ever read).

But whatever might have been the case during his own lifetime, the world has never stopped talking about Henry Adams since his death. Upon its release to the general public exactly six months after he died, the book which had aroused so much "publishing covetousness" in its future editor achieved, under the title *The Education of Henry Adams,* an even greater commercial and critical success than its record-breaking predecessor, *Mont-Saint-Michel and Chartres.* Today, both of these works of his old age, as well as most of his earlier ones, are still in print. Moreover, articles and books about Adams keep being produced at a rate that might have gratified even a vanity as large as his. In the last few years alone, for example, we have had one book (by Professor William Dusinberre) celebrating the major work of Adams's middle period, the nine-volume *History of the United States of America during the Administrations of Jefferson and Madison,* and another (a posthumously published study by the eminent critic R. P. Blackmur) treating Adams in general with almost as much reverence as he himself treated the Virgin Mary in *Mont-Saint-Michel and Chartres.* Now J. C. Levenson (the author of an earlier critical study of Adams), Ernest Samuels (whose authoritative three-volume biography of Adams was completed in 1964), and two other literary scholars (Charles Vandersee and Viola Hopkins Winner) have brought forth the first three volumes of a definitive edition of *The Letters of Henry Adams.*

Running altogether to nearly two thousand large and closely printed pages, these massive volumes take us from 1858 (when Adams was only twenty) to 1892, when he still had a quarter of a century to live. Three more volumes, of at least equivalent bulk, will therefore be required to complete the project. Yet so prolific a correspondent was Adams that not even the full six volumes will include all his extant letters. Of the 1,519 letters that have survived for the period covered by the first three volumes, "only" 1,277 have been included. Of these, nearly three-quarters have been published before, either in part or in full. The contribution of these volumes is thus 549 new letters and 261 complete texts of old letters previously available in abridged or expurgated form.

No doubt there are specialists who will think this contribution a significant one. But speaking as a general reader, I have to say that the work and the expense that went into this undertaking are not self-evidently justified by the results. First of all, anyone who approaches these letters more or less cold will find them very hard to follow. Adams in his early and middle years was not nearly so allusive and elliptical a stylist as he became toward the end of his life, but these letters are so crowded with people, events, and episodes about which even a reasonably well-informed reader today is bound to be either ignorant or vague that they are often impenetrable. Nor do the stingy little notes provided by the editors help much (though more expansive explication would admittedly have required a great deal of precious space). In addition to being obscure, many of these letters focus on details of little concern to anyone but students either of the period in question or of the life and career of Henry Adams. Finally, there is the problem of Adams's personality. There are very few people whose company would not become something of a strain after two thousand pages of letters, and Henry Adams is clearly not among them. Indeed, it is a tribute to his gifts as a writer that one can tolerate his tiresome affectations and poses, not to mention his nihilistic attitudes, even for a few hundred pages; but two thousand make an inhuman demand.

In saying all this, I do not mean to suggest that there is nothing of interest in Adams's letters, or that they are all impenetrable. Actually, to anyone who knows Adams only through the *Education*—which nowadays includes most of the people who know Adams at all—the letters he wrote in his youth are bound to come as a pleasant surprise. The author of *The Education of Henry Adams* was a disappointed man in his sixties, placing his great intellectual and literary powers entirely at the disposal of his bitterness. But the Henry Adams we encounter in the first volume of these letters was an exuberantly ambitious young man in his twenties, sufficiently sure of himself to think that the letters he was writing "might still be read and quoted as a memorial of manners and habits" a century or two later "when everything else about us is forgotten."

At the same time he was full of self-doubt and uncertainty about his future. Should he devote himself to the law or to politics or to literature? And whatever he might choose to do, was he good enough to uphold the Adams heritage and maintain the luster of the Adams name? Both his great-grandfather John Adams and his grandfather John Quincy Adams had, of course, been presidents of the United States, and it seemed entirely possible that his own father, Charles Francis Adams, might eventually follow them into the White House. The young Henry, as the third of Charles Francis's sons, felt crowded out of politics by his father and his older brothers (or so he said); as for the law, which upon graduating from Harvard he had gone to Germany to study, he soon decided that it was not for him, while he found himself attracted more and more by the idea of a literary career. "I read Gibbon," he informed his older brother Charles Francis Adams, Jr. (who had the highest regard for him). "Do you know, after long argument and reflexion I feel much as if perhaps some day I too might come to anchor like that. Our house needs a historian in this generation and I feel strongly tempted by the quiet and sunny prospect, while my ambition for political life dwindles as I get older" (this, at the age of twenty-two).

After his student year in Europe, during which Charles saw to the publication of some of his letters in a Boston paper, Henry moved to Washington where his father was serving in the House of Representatives. Again he wrote regularly to Charles in Boston, reporting in great detail on the intricate political maneuverings that preceded the outbreak of the Civil War. When the war finally came, Henry's father was appointed minister to England by the recently elected President Lincoln, and Henry went along as his private secretary. For the next seven years, he lived in London and now he reported to Charles and others on the intricate diplomatic maneuverings through which his father successfully prevented the British from openly siding with the Confederacy. With the example of Horace Walpole in mind, he also wrote a great many letters about the fashionable society of London and the country houses to which he had relatively easy access (while complaining that his status as an American aristocrat was not sufficiently appreciated by the British aristocrats among whom he moved).

These London letters, frankly written with an eye on posterity, have obviously succeeded in reaching their intended audience, but this does not mean that they succeeded in providing a vivid picture of the "manners and habits" of the time. Henry Adams had a powerful mind and he was a prose stylist of high distinction, but for all his relish of gossip he was no Walpole. Later, when he began writing narrative history, he demonstrated an ability to seize on the telling detail or the memorable anecdote, but, curiously, neither when writing letters nor when writing novels did he have command of that kind of eye. Often he went through the motions, describing balls and dinner parties, transcribing conversations, composing character sketches, and so on. Yet so lacking in spontaneity and so highly self-conscious were these exercises that for the most part they remained dead on the page. And there were occasions when he could hardly bring himself even to go through the motions: "Yesterday we had a pleasant dinner which the feminines will no doubt describe to you, at which Charles Dickens; John Forster, of 'Goldsmith' and the 'Statesman'; Louis Blanc, and other distinguished individuals, were present; and a very jolly dinner it was." So much for Adams as a chronicler of the life of his times.

In the second volume of this new edition of his letters, we follow Adams, now thirty, back to the United States, where he began publishing serious political essays on the corruptions and abuses of the Johnson and Grant administrations. This led to a joint appointment as editor of the *North American Review,* a quarterly journal that Adams proceeded to enlist in the cause of political reform, and as an assistant professor at Harvard, where he taught medieval history (a subject to which he would return later in life in *Mont-Saint-Michel and Chartres*). But during the seven years he spent at Harvard he also began thinking about and working on what would soon become his main preoccupation: the early history of his own country. It was during this period too that he met and married Marian Hooper (known as Clover).

In 1877 Adams left Cambridge for Washington, where his work as a historian began in earnest. Within an extraordinarily short time, he produced a scholarly biography of Jefferson's Secretary of the Treasury, Albert Gallatin; a more popular book about John Randolph, the great congressional prophet of southern secession; yet another about Aaron Burr (which was never published and has been lost); and two anonymously published novels, *Democracy* and *Esther*. At the same time, he worked steadily on his massive *History,* which involved tracking down and copying vast quantities of papers and documents from archives both in the United States and Europe.

His life in Washington, punctuated by much foreign travel, was as rich as it was productive. He was happily married to a woman who was considered by no less a judge than Henry James "one of the two most interesting women in America." He was surrounded by a loving circle of intimate friends like John Hay, the biographer of Lincoln and a future Secretary of State. He occupied a place at the very center of Washington society.

Not surprisingly, the letters Adams wrote during this, the most productive and happiest period of his life, were full of ebullience, optimism, and more good cheer than most readers of the *Education* would suspect him capable of. They were also considerably less self-conscious than his earlier letters and were largely addressed to the recipient rather than to posterity through the recipient. But like those earlier letters, they were crammed with details about current political activity of no great interest today—and also, incidentally, with even more tedious detail concerning his financial affairs, his shopping expeditions while traveling, and the building of a new house on Lafayette Square right across from the White House. Then, only days before moving into that house, "Clover" Adams, who had been in a depression since the recent death of her father, suddenly committed suicide. This great blow had a temporarily softening effect on Adams:

> During the last two weeks I have learned something more about life than I knew before, but the saddest discovery of all was that I did not stand alone in my extremity of suffering. The whole of society seemed to groan with the same anguish. My table was instantly covered with messages from

men and women whose own hearts were still aching with the same wounds, and who received me, with a new burst of their own sorrow, into their sad fraternity. My pain seemed lost in the immensity of human distress; and all these people were still carrying on their daily lives, as I must do.

Though from that moment forward he never stopped speaking of himself as a dead man undergoing a posthumous existence, Adams remained true to his resolution to carry on. He moved into his new house, he continued working on his *History,* and he went on a series of long journeys, first to Japan and then to the South Seas. Writing mainly to Elizabeth Cameron, a young married beauty with whom he carried on a (probably Platonic) affair for the rest of his life, Adams produced what amounted to a book on Samoa and Tahiti. But except perhaps for a brilliantly memorable series of portraits of Robert Louis Stevenson, these letters, making up the heart of Volume III, no more justify the claim that Adams was one of the great letter-writers in the English language than the earlier volumes do.

Nor do they justify another claim often made on behalf of Adams: that the great bitterness which increasingly became his most salient quality was caused in some sense by his wife's suicide. Adams certainly loved his wife, and he was undoubtedly crushed by her horrible death. But the liveliness and vitality of the letters he wrote to Elizabeth Cameron so shortly afterward—not to mention his great passion for her—suggest that he recovered much more quickly and fully than he had expected or than some, who have taken his extravagant rhetoric at face value, believe.

Was it then America that made Henry Adams bitter? Here, after all, was a man descended from the most distinguished political family in American history and richly endowed in his own right; yet so bad had things evidently become in the America of his day that he could find no proper role to play in its political life. This was the view Adams himself took of his own case in the *Education,* and the last time I looked closely at him and his work, which was about twenty-five years ago, I saw no reason to question it. For in expressing his disgust with what had been happening to America in the decades after the Civil War, Adams was entirely at one with the standard diagnosis of the "Gilded Age," when (according to what *my* education had taught me to believe) the whole country was being ruined by reckless commercialism and political corruption. Moreover, in saying that he was "heavily handicapped . . . in running for such stakes as the century had to offer," he was proclaiming his membership in the community of those whose very virtues of mind and character had unfitted them for success in the kind of society America had become. This was the society that—or so almost every twentieth-century literary critic since the days of Van Wyck Brooks had been arguing— stifled the genius of Mark Twain and drove Henry James into exile, while exalting "robber barons" like Jay Gould and John D. Rockefeller and the venal politicians whom they bought and sold at will. In such a society there was no place for a patrician idealist like Henry Adams.

Nor was Adams an isolated case. According to Edmund Wilson, himself a product of the patriciate:

> The period after the Civil War—both banal in a bourgeois way and fantastic with gigantic fortunes—was a difficult one for Americans brought up in the old tradition. . . . They had been educated at Exeter and Andover and at eighteenth-century Princeton, and had afterwards been trained, like their fathers, for what had once been called the learned professions; but they had then had to deal with a world in

which this kind of education and the kind of ideals it served no longer really counted for much.

In speaking here of his father's generation, Wilson was echoing the ideas and even the language of Adams's *Education*. To be sure, Wilson found Adams a much less sympathetic victim than John Jay Chapman, another patrician writer of the same generation who (in Wilson's words) inflicted "permanent psychological damage" on himself "by beating his head against the gilt of the Gilded Age." (Chapman, incidentally, was no great admirer of Adams either—"the piping Adams as he sits on his raft in the sunset and combs his golden hair with a golden toothpick.") But the qualities Wilson disliked in Adams—his coldness and his malice—were, as Wilson's friend F. Scott Fitzgerald might have said, merely personal. Adams remained for Wilson a victim of the politics of the period. And for many others, he became, and has remained to this day, one of the main counts in an indictment of America as a country entirely given over to commercialism, philistinism, and corruption.

Having absorbed and accepted this general view for so long, I was taken aback by what I found when I began reading Adams again a few months ago. To start with, what struck me this time more forcibly than before was how bitter Adams was from his earliest days. Even as a high-spirited young man—and long before the world could have given him any cause—he suffered from what he himself would later call "moral dyspepsia." He had a decidedly sour attitude toward most of the people he met while a student in Germany and then when working for his father in London; he disliked most of the European capitals he visited, including Berlin, Paris, and Rome (which he would later adore); and even in his twenties and thirties, his natural vitality was already subject to corrosion by frequent bouts of anxiety and self-pity.

The second thing that struck me in returning to Adams was the ferocity of his ambition. What he wanted above all else was success, and he wanted it in all the usual forms: power, money, status, acclaim. As an Adams, he was expected to seek power—not, to be sure, for its own sake, but in order to serve some higher good. Yet he never had a very clear sense of what this higher good might be. At first, he believed in civil-service reform, in the gold standard, in laissez-faire, and in free trade. Later he changed his mind about gold and several other issues. But reading his letters and his books, one comes away with the strong feeling that particular issues were beside the point; Adams simply assumed that the higher good would be served if he and people like him were running the country. "We want a national set of young men like ourselves or better," he wrote from London to Charles, "to start new influences not only in politics, but in literature, in law, in society, and throughout the whole social organism of the country—a national school of our own generation. . . ."

Adams himself never held public office, high or low, and according to R. P. Blackmur, his "failure in American political society" was not due to any incapacity of his own but rather to "society's inability to make use of him: its inability to furnish a free field for intelligent political action." In the past, there had been such a field but America was now "bound for quick success. . . . It cared nothing for political mastery, and commonly refused to admit it had a purpose beyond the aggregation of force in the form of wealth."

Now, as it happens, Henry Adams himself, as his letters clearly showed, was not above dreaming of quick success. Nor could any reader of these letters, with their incessant harping on his investments and those of his family and friends, think that he was indifferent to the accumulation of wealth. George Santayana, for one, came away from a visit to Adams with the opposite impression:

> "So you are trying to teach philosophy at Harvard," Mr. Adams said. . . . "I once tried to teach history there, but it can't be done. It isn't really possible to teach anything." This . . . was not encouraging. Still . . . Mr. Adams's house . . . [was] luxurious. I got the impression that, if most things were illusions, having money and spending money were great realities.

Be that as it may, there is plenty of reason for dismissing the idea that Adams's failure to realize his political ambitions proved that American society had become too crass and too fixated on wealth to make use of its best-bred, best-educated, and most talented young men. For one thing, a good many other young men with backgrounds similar to Adams's, and with exactly the same education that supposedly incapacitated him, did manage to enter American political life in his time and to make an enormous mark. One of them was Henry Cabot Lodge—the descendant of a family almost as eminent as the Adamses, a former student of Henry Adams himself at Harvard and his junior colleague on the *North American Review,* a distinguished author, and in general a person of great intellectual gifts—who became perhaps the most important senator of the age. Another was Theodore Roosevelt, who, like Adams, came of patrician stock and was also an author of no small accomplishment (among many other books he wrote a four-volume history, *The Winning of the West*). And if Lodge and Roosevelt succeeded in electoral politics, Oliver Wendell Holmes (another Harvard friend and colleague) was appointed to the Supreme Court, while John Hay (Adams's closest friend) was able to become Secretary of State.

The careers of men like these obviously demonstrate that Adams was incapacitated, not by his education, his background, or his intellect, but by his lack of the qualities necessary to political success in a democracy—most especially the willingness to subject himself to the judgment and the control of ordinary people. For all their high-mindedness and their fears of "King Demos," John Adams and John Quincy Adams had this willingness, and their descendant Henry Adams did not. So fastidious was he that he refused to associate with anyone outside the smallest and most select of circles, whether social or intellectual. ("Hang it," says a character Henry James modeled on Adams, "let us be vulgar and have some fun—let us invite the President," while John Jay Chapman once commented that Adams was a member of "the Secret Society of the Only Intellectuals in America.") As if this were not enough, Adams was so sensitive to criticism that he could hardly bear to publish his books for fear that they would be exposed to the judgment of an ignorant tribe of reviewers. The idea that such a man could run for office in any democratic society at any time, or even do the demeaning things that are usually required to put oneself in the way of appointive office, is simply ridiculous (as anyone who has read *Coriolanus* should know).

This, at any rate, is what several of his own friends thought. "If the country had put him on a pedestal," Oliver Wendell Holmes once remarked to Owen Wister, "I think Henry Adams with his gifts could have rendered distinguished public service." When Wister asked, "What was the matter with Henry Adams?" Holmes replied, "He wanted it handed to him on a silver platter." And in an unmistakable allusion to Adams in the course of a comment about John Hay, Theodore Roosevelt observed that Hay's "temptation was to associate as far as possible only with men of refined and cultivated tastes, who lived apart from the world of affairs, and who, if Americans, were wholly lacking in robustness of fibre."

Sensing all this about himself, Adams never even tried to make a political career. But withdrawing from politics did not mean giving up on ambition. On the contrary, telling himself that political power was "the most barren of all forms of success," while literature offered "higher prizes than politics," he decided to concentrate on the writing of history. In this area too his ambition knew no bounds. If he could not be worthy of the family name by getting into the White House, he would travel to glory by an even better route: he would become the successor of Gibbon and the American Macaulay.

In dreaming this dream of greatness, at least, Adams was reaching for something that he had both the character and the endowment to achieve. He was a brilliant writer; he was a patient, scrupulous, and indefatigable scholar; and his talent for observing the world of affairs was as keen as his ability to live in it was poor (for, as Henry James remarked of the character based on Adams, though he might not have been in politics, "politics were much in him").

Ten years he spent on his *History,* and when the nine volumes were finally completed and published, the results came as a hideous disappointment. The reviews were on the whole respectful, but no one acclaimed him as the new Gibbon or the Macaulay of America. And whereas both Gibbon and Macaulay had sold in the tens of thousands, Adams's sales (about which he cared desperately) were very modest.

Here then was a double disappointment. Having turned to literature with an uneasy conscience—for he never could rid himself of the feeling that as an Adams he was supposed to be in politics—but having persuaded himself that literary success was, after all, better, he failed to achieve even that, at least in his own eyes. It was bad enough that America had frustrated his political ambitions, but it was worse still that it refused to make even his literary dreams come true. And so Adams's alienation was now complete—so much so that William Phillips, the editor of *Partisan Review,* for whom the condition of alienation was the true mark of the American intellectual, could by 1941 see in him "a symbol of our entire culture."

That Adams was alienated from the America of his day is certainly true, but it has been too easily assumed that the estrangement was entirely the result—or rather the fault—of the changes that came over the country in the Gilded Age. Quite apart from the issue of whether Adams would have been any more at home in the society of his ancestors, there is also a question to be raised about the putative decline of America from their time to his own. In this connection it is interesting to note that, as we learn from Adams himself, the very same charges had been made against the supposedly pure precapitalist America of 1800 as were now being made against the America of the Gilded Age. In "The United States in 1800," the long prologue to his *History,* Adams wrote:

> In the foreigner's range of observation, love of money was the most conspicuous and most common trait of American character. . . . No foreigner of that day—neither poet, painter, nor philosopher—could detect in American life anything higher than vulgarity. . . . Englishmen especially indulged in unbounded invective against the sordid character of American society. . . . Contemporary critics could see neither generosity, economy, honor, nor ideas of any kind in the American breast. . . . [Even Wordsworth] could do no better, when he stood in the face of American democracy, than "keep the secret of a poignant scorn."

Dismissing the idea that the critics might have been right, Adams insisted that their contempt for America showed nothing more than an astonishing lack of imagination. "Wordsworth might have convinced himself by a moment's thought that no country could act on the imagination as America acted upon the instincts of the ignorant and poor, without some quality that deserved better treatment than poignant scorn." Indeed, though the philosophers and the poets could see only rapacity and vulgarity in America, "the poorest peasant in Europe" could discern "the dim outline of a mountain-summit across the ocean, rising high above the mist and mud of American democracy." Adams went even further:

> . . . the hard, practical, money-getting American democrat, who had neither generosity nor honor nor imagination, and who inhabited cold shades where fancy sickened and where genius died, was in truth living in a world of dream, and acting a drama more instinct with poetry than all the avatars of the east, walking in gardens of emerald and rubies, in ambition already ruling the world and guiding Nature with a kinder and wiser hand than had ever yet been felt in human history.

Every word of this could be applied with equal, perhaps even greater, force to much of what was written by Adams himself and so many others about the materialism, corruption, and philistinism of America in the Gilded Age, when new waves of immigrant masses were pouring into the country, encouraged by a new breed of "American speculator" inviting them (as Adams said their forebears of 1800 had also done) to "Come and share our limitless riches! Come and help us bring to light these unimaginable stores of wealth and power!"

In short, in speaking of the America of 1880, Adams

sounded exactly like the foreign critics he had derided for their blindness to the poetry of the America of 1800, even though most of the changes that had taken place during those eighty years (including the abolition of slavery) had, if anything, been for the better. Nor was Adams blind only to the political and economic "poetry" of his own time; he was also dead to its poetry in the more literal sense. For example, he rarely read and had no appreciation for the novels of his lifelong friend Henry James. "There is no thought in America," he said at a time when William James and John Dewey, among others, were active. Nor did he have any interest in contemporary American painters like Eakins and Whistler (or for that matter in the French Impressionists, and he positively hated such European writers of the day as Hardy, Ibsen, and Zola).

This alienation from the life of his own time found negative expression in increasingly violent private outbursts and in various "scientific" theories according to which the whole world was in a state of inexorable decline; "the huge eternal cataclysm" was surely coming within fifty years and his only fear was that he would not live to see it. These apocalyptic yearnings were, moreover, invariably accompanied by anti-Semitic outbursts so frenzied that they scandalized even some of his friends. During the Dreyfus Affair, John Hay (no great philo-Semite himself) said that Adams "now believes the earthquake at Krakatoa was the work of Zola and when he saw Vesuvius reddening the midnight air he searched the horizon to find a Jew stoking the fire." But Hay's description, with all its humorous extravagance, caught only the obsessiveness of Adams's hatred of Jews, not the virulence that came out in such remarks as: "The Jew has got into the soul. I see him—or her—now everywhere, and wherever he—or she—goes, there must remain a taint in the blood forever." Or again: "I tell you Rome was a blessed garden of paradise beside the rotten, unsexed, swindling, lying Jews, represented by Pierpont Morgan and the gang who have been manipulating the country for the last few years." Or again: "I am myself more than ever at odds with my time. I detest it and everything that belongs to it, and live only in the wish to see the end of it, with all its infernal Jewry. . . . I want to go to India, and be a Brahmin, and worship a monkey."

Instead of going to India, however, Adams went to the South Seas to romanticize the primitive culture of Samoa and Tahiti and to lament its impending ruination by Western influence. And instead of becoming a Brahmin and worshiping a monkey, he became (in imagination at least) a Christian of the thirteenth century and worshiped the Virgin Mary. In *Mont-Saint-Michel and Chartres,* Adams's nihilism gave way for the moment to reverence, as a lyrical talent for celebration which had been dormant since the completion of his *History* was reawakened by the cathedrals, the poetry, and the philosophy of medieval France. But the old Adams, so to speak, soon returned to write the *Education,* and here his nihilism, refined into a prose of subtly poisonous elegance and density, informed almost every word. For if the thirteenth century represented civilization at its height and called for reverence, the twentieth century was the culmination of a long process of degradation and degeneration to which the only sensible response was vindictive raillery. As to this invidious contrast, perhaps the best comment was made by Yvor Winters in his long essay on Adams:

Adams arrived at his view of the middle ages by concentrating on a few great products of literature, thought, and architecture; ignoring everything else, he asserted that these were the thirteenth century. He arrived at his view of the twentieth century by reversing the process. He thus deduced that the world was deteriorating, and so found a justification for his own state of mind.

What then remains of Adams today? Despite the best efforts of his epigones and his apologists, the *Education* is still the only one of Adams's books that is generally regarded as an indispensable classic. Some critics, Winters among them, consider the *History* a great work, but there is no use pretending that anyone other than a specialist in the period is ever going to read nine volumes covering only seventeen years of early American history. On the other hand, the prologue and epilogue, which together make up a manageable book, can still be read with great pleasure and profit. The same cannot be said of the biographies of Gallatin and Randolph; for the general reader, they are at best curiosities, while of the perfunctory little book Adams produced on the poet George Cabot Lodge (the last thing he ever wrote) not even that much can be said. Unlike Winters, I find much that is beautiful and illuminating in *Mont-Saint-Michel and Chartres,* but so technical and so hermetic is it, especially in the long sections on architecture, that only someone with a special reason for doing so is likely to pick it up or to stay with it until the end (even Edmund Wilson, who read everything, could never bring himself to read it). As for Adams's novels, *Democracy* (an exposé of the corruptions of Washington in the era of Grant and Hayes) is a mildly interesting document, but it has no value as a work of art, and *Esther* (which deals in the standard terms of the period with the conflict between science and religion) is an embarrassingly poor performance altogether.

We come back, then, to the *Education,* which many profess to regard as a great work, but which to me now seems repellent in its hostility, its self-pity, and what Wilson called its "stealthy and elusive malice." It is also so arch and elliptical that I wonder how many of its admirers have been able to follow it any better thar William James did. It was, James complained, "a hodge-podge of world fact, private fact, philosophy, irony," and he told Adams that "A great deal of the later diplomatic history is dealt with so much by hint and implication that to an ignoramus like W. J. it reads obscurely."

In the early 1950s, when the reputation of Adams had fallen in proportion to the new (and short-lived) enthusiasm among literary intellectuals for "our country and our culture," Lionel Trilling cautioned against reading "Adams permanently out of our intellectual life." Trilling acknowledged that there was much to be said against Adams—and he himself said it all—but there were moments when we needed him:

> We are at one with Adams whenever our sense of the American loneliness and isolation becomes especially strong, whenever we feel that our culture belongs to everyone except ourselves and our friends, whenever we believe that our talents and our devotion are not being sufficiently used.

This is an acute diagnosis of Adams's appeal, but there is another way of putting the same point. Thus one can say that Adams has been kept alive as an incitement to and a justification of the hunger of the American intellectual class for the power, and especially the political power, that he himself, for all that he denigrated it, could never stop wanting and envying. The life of the mind was never enough for Adams, and if he is an exemplary figure, what he exemplifies is the self-hatred so many American writers and thinkers have felt over being "mere" intellectuals, and the self-pity they have experienced over what they have taken to be their own powerlessness.

The great irony is that the case of Adams—who remains a force when the names of Rutherford B. Hayes or Chester Arthur are scarcely even remembered—demonstrates how much more powerful intellectuals can be in the long run than even the most successful of politicians. This does not, however, mean that Adams is a force for good. On the contrary, in encouraging a bigoted contempt for this country and in subtly denigrating and devaluing the life of the mind, he has exerted so malignant an influence that, unlike Trilling, I see little of value that would be lost by allowing him to slip into the obscurity he so often boasted of wishing to achieve.

6.

THE ADVERSARY CULTURE
AND THE NEW CLASS

Among the many puzzles thrown up by the disruptions of the 1960s in the United States, none seemed more perplexing than the virulent hostility toward their own country which was evidently felt by some of the most privileged elements of American society. That blacks should resent or even be enraged by American society seemed entirely understandable and, indeed, proper. Having been victimized for so long by discrimination, poverty, and lack of opportunity, they had good reason to protest, to demonstrate, to disrupt. But what reason did undergraduates at Berkeley, Columbia, and Harvard have for feeling the same way and engaging in the same kind of behavior? Why should young people from prosperous families who had been given—as the saying used to go—"every advantage," who were enjoying what to all outward appearances was a life of luxury, indulgence, and ease, and who could look forward with relative assurance to positions of comparable status and reward in the years ahead, characterize themselves as "niggers"? ("The Student as Nigger" was actually the title of a widely circulated manifesto of the period.) In what intelligible sense could these young scions of the American upper classes be compared to a group at the bottom of the American heap?

Such talk of "the student as nigger" might have been dismissed as a particularly flamboyant form of adolescent self-dramatization if not for another perplexing fact: that it was ratified by very large numbers of people in the adult world, including, as it sometimes seemed, the entire membership of the academic and journalistic professions. Far from ridiculing the idea that the prosperous and privileged young of America in reality constituted an oppressed and downtrodden minority, sociologists and editorialists, foundation executives and columnists were busily at work generating arguments to prove that the contention was sound. These adult apologists, who kept telling us what the young people were "trying to tell us" (though their services in this respect often struck one as supererogatory), were, moreover, a privileged group themselves, occupying for the most part extremely well-paid positions to which great influence and considerable prestige were attached. Why should they be as hostile to America as the words they kept putting into the mouths of the "young" so clearly suggested they were?

Throughout the years roughly bounded by the end of the Civil War and the beginning of the Second World War, no one would have been surprised to find intellectuals* and aspiring intellectuals expressing hostility toward American society. With the rapid industrial expansion of the country

---

* The term is, of course, notoriously difficult to define. I use it to mean people professionally, or anyway passionately, concerned with the study, propagation, and dissemination of ideas, attitudes, and ideologies. Usually such people have been exposed to a university education, but this is not a necessary condition. Sometimes they are very intelligent, but that is not a necessary condition either.

in the decades after the Civil War, America more and more
became the quintessential "business civilization"—a society
in which tremendous power of every kind was vested in the
business class. But as this power grew, and as the abuses
flowing so abundantly from its exercise accumulated, resistance to it also developed. Antitrust laws, progressive in-
come taxes, regulatory legislation, electoral reform, and the
rise of organized labor—all were directed at diminishing or
at least controlling the rampant economic and political
power of the "robber barons," of "Wall Street," of the trusts
and the monopolies. Efforts of this nature were supported
by rival economic groups—farmers, small-town merchants,
independent professionals, and manual workers—whose interests were threatened and often trampled upon by big
business, and who attacked the new order of things in the
name of values like free competition and equality of opportunity, which big business itself, of course, also honored (if
more in the breach than in the observance).

At the same time, however, a more radical assault on the
new order was also being mounted, which in the long run
perhaps proved more decisive. It was an assault directed
against the spiritual and cultural power of business—that is,
against the very values that the populists and the Progres-
sives and the labor movement shared with big business and
to which they appealed in their own struggle for a greater
share of political and economic power. In this cultural
battle, the weapons used were not political, and progress was
not measured in legislative victories. The relevant weapons
were ideas and the object was to persuade and influence.
Nor was the point to expose the injustices flowing from a
business civilization (or a capitalist system, as some Americans later learned to call it); the emphasis here fell on
spiritual rather than material considerations. Of course,
separating the spiritual from the material was not always

possible or desirable. Nevertheless, there did develop a critique of capitalist America which centered independently
on what in our own day is known as the "quality of life."
Indeed, so vivid an autonomous existence did this critique
achieve that it retained its plausibility even at a time when
the strictly economic arguments against the system (the
Marxist ones, among others) seemed to have been refuted
by the spread of affluence to unprecedentedly large numbers
of people.

This cultural critique consisted essentially of three related
elements. First of all, it was said that a society in which
business was the leading species of enterprise put a premium
on selfishness while doing everything it could to dampen the
altruistic potentialities of human nature. People were rewarded for being selfish and penalized for caring about
others; they were encouraged to compete instead of to
cooperate. The result was an erosion of communal attach-
ments and loyalties, and the creation of a harsh, brutal,
heartless society of isolated individuals connected one to the
other by a "cash nexus" and nothing more lasting or
binding.

In addition to encouraging the worst kind of "rugged
individualism," a business civilization, it was charged, stim-
ulated the basest of human passions—material greed. The
lust for money and for the things money could buy became
so ferocious that more elevated tastes were forced to go beg-
ging for satisfaction. People grew narrow and gross, in-
capable of appreciating anything whose value could not be
counted in dollars. The arts were thus meaningless to them,
or at best a showy adornment pressed into the service of
an ostentatious vulgarity. And just as individuals living
under such circumstances were related only by a "cash
nexus," so their only religion was worship (in William
James's phrase) of "the bitch-goddess SUCCESS."

These attacks on the individualism, materialism, and philistinism of a business civilization were rooted in Christianity and derived a good part of their effectiveness from the continuing strength, sometimes latent, sometimes active, of Christian belief in the United States. But there was a third element of the critique which was rooted in secular and even anti-Christian sources, and this was the attack on the puritanism of "bourgeois" or "middle-class" society. Such a society, it was said, while rewarding the lust for money, penalized all the healthier appetites. The only pleasures it sanctioned were whatever pleasures might be connected with work, ambition, the sense of having "made it" or won out in a brutal competitive struggle. All other pleasures, whether of the mind or of the body, were frowned upon as wicked or as debilitating or as a waste of precious time. A life lived under the rule of these values was stern, joyless, desiccated, prissy, provincial, repressed.

In elaborating this critique, intellectuals—and especially intellectuals primarily interested in the arts—quite naturally played the leading role. For the very act of becoming an intellectual or an artist in America* came to mean that one was in effect joining the party of opposition—placing oneself (to use the term made famous by Lionel Trilling in *Beyond Culture*) in an "adversary" relation to the business civilization and all its works. To be sure, some of these "works"

---

* This is not to imply that the attitudes of the adversary culture were indigenous or peculiar to America. Similar stories could be told of all the industrial countries. But there were important differences between Europe and America in this as in so many other areas. For example, in Europe opposition to the rising power of industrial capitalism came (at least until 1945) from the Right as well as the Left, taking the form of fascism and of literally reactionary political movements which advocated the restoration of monarchy or of an essentially feudal social organization. Although major American writers living in Europe like T. S. Eliot and Ezra Pound were among the sympathizers of these movements, nothing really comparable materialized in the United States, possibly because this country had no feudal past.

to which most American partisans of the adversary culture were opposed (though there were such prominent exceptions as William Faulkner) included values like religious piety, patriotism, and the martial virtues that derived not from capitalism but from precapitalist roots: the ethos of the rural community and the small town. But as was evident from the term "booboisie" invented by H. L. Mencken to suggest an identification between the "hick" of the hinterland and the businessman (wherever he might live and however large or small his business), the two tended to flow together in the adversary American mind into a single enemy.

Nor did membership in the adversary culture merely involve subscribing to abstract doctrines critical of bourgeois society; it also involved matters of style and sensibility. Thus the "modernist" movement which began sweeping through all the arts around the turn of the century and which was characterized above all else by an unremitting impulse toward formal experimentation—Ezra Pound's "make it new!" was the great slogan—represented something more than an effort to escape from played-out aesthetic conventions and to find fresher forms of expression and interpretation. There was in this movement a powerful will to *épater le bourgeois,* to provoke and outrage the middle-class audience by upsetting its normal expectations and offending its sense of intelligibility, fitness, and order. While very often attacking or ridiculing the bourgeois world in substantive terms (through, for example, unflattering portraits and characterizations), the modernist movement was simultaneously mounting an assault on the very structure of its sensibility. Indeed, Edmund Wilson in his book on the Symbolists, *Axel's Castle,* went so far as to suggest that the modernist revolution in the arts was analogous both in purpose and significance to the Russian Revolution: as the one represented a challenge to the rule of the bourgeoisie in the world of politics, the other represented a challenge to its rule in the world of imagination and ideas.

That modernist or avant-garde artists and their critical partisans should stand in an adversary relation to bourgeois society was to be expected almost by definition. But in America even artists and intellectuals like Theodore Dreiser or Van Wyck Brooks who were opposed on aesthetic grounds to modernism shared fully in its attitude toward the business civilization. Until, that is, the Second World War and its aftermath. While business as such continued to be treated with contempt throughout the 1940s and 1950s—this was the period of books like *The Organization Man* and *The Man in the Gray Flannel Suit* which amounted to nothing more than updated and popularized versions of the cultural critique—a new and more positive attitude toward American society itself, and even toward the capitalist system, began to emerge among artists and intellectuals. Those who participated in and applauded this surprising phenomenon said that as compared with the alternatives of Nazi Germany on the one side and Soviet Russia on the other, America looked very good to them— especially since "countervailing forces," as John Kenneth Galbraith called them, had by now cut into the power of big business and made for a more pluralistic cultural climate and one more hospitable to values other than those of commerce. Those who deplored this development said that the intellectuals were simply "selling out" for good jobs and a better social position, and that we were faced with the onset of a new "age of conformity."

Such worries, as we now know, were misplaced. The first postwar decade turned out to be not the beginning of a new "age of conformity"—that is, of amity between the intellectuals and American society—but a temporary aberration, destined to be corrected, and with a vengeance, in the decade ahead. To journalists and popular sociologists with short historical memories, this correction looked like a novel development. It was not; it was a return to the traditional stance of the intellectual community in relation to American society.

There was, however, one truly novel element in the situation of the sixties: the vastly enlarged numbers of people who now either belonged to the intellectual community or were under its direct influence. In the past intellectuals had constituted a tiny minority of the population, but with the tremendous expansion of higher education in the period after World War II, millions upon millions of young people began to be exposed to—one might even say indoctrinated in—the adversary culture of the intellectuals. To be sure, very few of these young people actually became intellectuals in any real sense, but a great many were deeply influenced by ideas which had once been confined pretty much to the intellectual community itself. Thus what had formerly been the attitudes of a minuscule group on the margins of American society now began assuming the proportions of a veritable mass movement. And since so many of these young people eventually wound up working in the mass media, such attitudes acquired a new ability to penetrate into previously inaccessible areas of American culture.

But if this history helps to explain why so much hostility to American society was to be found in the sixties among intellectuals and their students, and in the mass media, it does not tell us why the adversary culture should have returned with so great a force precisely at a time when intellectuals not only had less personal reason than ever before to resent American society, but also when the doctrines of the adversary culture itself had become less plausible as a description of American society than ever before.

After all, in the heyday of bourgeois self-confidence—during the Gilded Age of the 1870s and 1880s, or even during the boom of the 1920s—when people who had "never met a payroll" were held in contempt, when artists and intellectuals were often unable to earn a living, when works of the mind and spirit were either ridiculed or ignored, when originality and experimentation in the arts were derided and even persecuted—under these circumstances it would have been amazing if artists and intellectuals had responded with anything but an answering bitterness and hostility.

But conditions were very different by the 1960s. If in the past artists and intellectuals had been despised as compared with businessmen, they were now more and more being held in generally high esteem. They were honored, they were consulted, they were even envied for doing more important work and living more interesting lives than people engaged in the pursuit of material gain. If in the past it had been difficult or even impossible for artists and intellectuals to support themselves by writing or painting or composing, an increasing number were now finding new ways of managing. There were jobs—relatively well-paying jobs—at universities, there were grants to be had from foundations, and most important of all there was a new and responsive public growing up, ready to listen to the things they had to say and to buy (often at huge prices) the things they had to sell. And if in the past originality and experimentation in art and thought had encountered tremendous resistance, they were by now being welcomed as fervently as they had once been rejected. Stories and articles by "highbrow" writers like Saul Bellow, Harold Rosenberg, and Mary McCarthy were printed in such mass magazines as *Life, Playboy,* and the *Saturday Evening Post,* while books which had once been considered virtually unpublishable (Paul Goodman's *Growing Up Absurd,* for example) were appearing on best-seller lists. Paperback reprints of difficult modernist works which only yesterday had been regarded as beyond the pale were enjoying huge sales and were being taught as classics in schools and colleges. And there were similar developments in the worlds of painting, sculpture, music, theater, and dance, where the avant-garde became so powerful and so fashionable that all other styles were either deprived of cultural respectability or were altogether driven out. Despite its continuing sense of itself as engaged in a heroic battle against the philistine bourgeois world, the avant-garde, Hilton Kramer said in his definitive study, *The Age of the Avant-Garde,* had become *the* establishment, the country's most powerful cultural force.

Given this new situation, one might have expected the adversary culture to lose its bite or perhaps even to disappear—killed, as it were, by kindness. And yet exactly the opposite occurred. Beginning in the late 1950s, what one sympathetic observer has called "a second wave of modernism" began gathering force which was, if anything, even more virulent in its hatred of bourgeois or middle-class society than the first one had been. Listening to these latter-day epigoni of the modernist revolution, one might have thought that nothing had changed except for the worse. America, they said, and in the most strident tones, was still dominated by business and its values, and those values were still as grounded in materialism, philistinism, and puritanism as they had been in the past. Life in the "establishment" (in this usage a category which came to include virtually anyone who worked for a living, but never the speaker himself, no matter how successful in the worldly sense he might be) was a "rat race"; the only purpose of such a life was the consumption of material goods which grew ever tackier and more useless; it was a boring life, a sterile "air-conditioned nightmare" lacking in vitality, spontaneity, or the capacity for sexual satisfaction. One of the first of the new modernists, Jack Kerouac, summed it all up in his novel *On the Road* as "millions and millions, hustling forever for a buck among themselves . . . grabbing, taking, giving, sighing, dying."

Yet the very success which writers who took this point of view began to enjoy in the late fifties belied their claim that nothing had changed and that America was still dominated by business and its values. For paradoxically nothing was better calculated to win the applause of the "establishment" than denunciations of it. The publication of *On the Road* itself, for example, was hailed by a reviewer in the *New York Times* (then still in its old incarnation and still called "the good gray *Times*") as "a historic occasion," and Kerouac became a nationwide celebrity. So did many other writers associated with him in the Beat Generation, especially Allen Ginsberg who declared in his poem "Howl" that the "best minds" of his generation had literally been driven mad by life in middle-class America. And so, ultimately, did dozens upon dozens of their followers and successors—novelists, poets, playwrights, film-makers, social critics, journalists, and rock and pop musicians—who were rewarded with riches, fame, and adulation for heaping contempt and ridicule on the society around them.

The reason, then, that the adversary culture was not killed by kindness is that it was encouraged by kindness. Tocqueville points out that the French Revolution—the revolution of the bourgeoisie against the aristocracy—erupted out of an improving rather than a worsening situation. As the power and confidence of the middle class increased, so did its appetite and hence also its animosity toward the *ancien régime*. Is it too fanciful to apply the same analysis to the intellectual class in America in the 1960s? Certainly it did not seem too fanciful to many of the intellectuals themselves.

During the sixties, a theory began to circulate to the effect that a "New Class" was maturing in America made up of persons whose "capital" consisted not of money or property but of education, brains, and technical expertise—intellectuals, in the broadest sense—and that in an advanced stage of capitalist development such as the United States was now reaching, this New Class would eventually replace the old owners and entrepreneurs—that is, the bourgeoisie—as the ruling elite.

In this "liberal" variant of the theory (propounded by writers as diverse as Daniel Bell, David T. Bazelon, and John Kenneth Galbraith) the intellectuals were seen as the beneficiaries of an orderly transfer of power destined to take place as the byproduct of structural changes in the economic organization of the system. But there was another variant— a radical or neo-Marxist one (whose most prominent proponent was probably C. Wright Mills). In that version the intellectuals were seen as the agents of revolution, replacing the proletariat, the class that Marx had cast in this role but that had evidently traded its historic birthright for a mess of affluent pottage.

Whether in its liberal or its neo-Marxist version, the dream of power seems to have acted upon the intellectuals as Tocqueville says the same dream acted upon the bourgeoisie in prerevolutionary France: it sharpened the appetite and exacerbated hostility to the tottering and doddering ruling class of the old regime which so stubbornly insisted on postponing the inevitable with one stratagem after another. Thus if in an earlier period bourgeois society was hated because it ignored and despised the intellectuals, now it was hated because, despite all the concessions it had made, it still refused to be *ruled* by the intellectuals.

Only once before in the post-Civil War period had American intellectuals seriously entertained so ambitious a vision for themselves, and that was in the early years of the Great Depression. Up until that time, the practical strategy followed by the adversary culture was generally to withdraw entirely from political activity. For the grip of the business class seemed so firm that one was reduced to railing from the sidelines in the manner of Henry Adams—who, as we have seen, conducted a species of ideological guerrilla warfare against the new political order in America—or turning one's back in self-destructive despair. To quote again from Edmund Wilson's description of the young patricians of his father's generation who had been "brought up in the old tradition," with its ideals of public service: "Of my father's close friends at college, but a single one was left by the time he was in his thirties; all the rest were dead— some had committed suicide. . . . My father had in his youth aimed at public life. . . . But he could not . . . be induced to take part in the kind of political life that he knew at the end of the century."*

There did, however, emerge an alternative to the course followed by Henry Adams on the one side and the elder Wilson and his friends on the other, which Edmund Wilson himself and many of his own friends adopted: emigration, either literally to Paris or London where the atmosphere seemed more congenial and more hospitable, or figuratively to a "bohemian" community in which the values of the adversary culture were turned into the prevailing norm. In such communities—the most famous sprang up in the early years of the century in New York's Greenwich Village—it was the artistic vocation and the life of the mind to which

* The pathos here is a little exaggerated, since the elder Wilson *was* "induced to take part" in public life to the extent of serving a term as attorney-general of New Jersey in the administration of Governor Woodrow Wilson (no relation). Throughout the past century, patricians (with a few glaring exceptions like the two Roosevelts) have characteristically been much less successful at getting elected to public office than at being appointed to it.

everyone aspired, and business that everyone despised; in such communities there was (at least in theory) mutual encouragement and solidarity instead of ruthless competition; and in such communities puritanism and its institutional embodiments—chastity, monogamy, the family—were laughed at, and everyone believed in freedom, spontaneity, self-expression, and the pleasures of the flesh.

In such communities, in short, those who were "alienated" from the spiritual "wasteland" into which the business class allegedly had turned their country—those who had metaphorically been left homeless and driven into internal exile—could find a haven and a new home. It went without saying that in such communities everyone was more or less a socialist, or an anarchist, or a pacifist, or even (though more rarely) a monarchist or a fascist—anything but a Republican or a Democrat. But it also went without saying that these political sentiments carried with them very little expectation of being translated into actual political power. Someday, but certainly not now, things would change out there in America, but certainly not yet.

Then came the crash of 1929 and the Great Depression, and suddenly the opportunity for carrying the fight against the power of business directly into the political arena looked amazingly good. Thus Edmund Wilson, who had in any case been growing disturbed throughout the twenties by the thought that withdrawal from contemporary political struggles by intellectuals amounted to a complacent acquiescence in the rule of the business class, joined with Sherwood Anderson, John Dos Passos, Granville Hicks, Malcolm Cowley, and other important literary figures in an appeal to their fellow writers to vote for the Communist ticket in the 1932 presidential elections, specifically on the ground that the depression offered the first good chance since the Gilded Age to take the country away from the businessman. In order to do this the intellectuals would of course have to forge an alliance with the working class, which Wilson and his colleagues still imagined to be represented by the Communist party. But the end result would be a society in which "the power of the spirit" would at last prevail against the gilt of all Gilded Ages. It would be a society, in other words, run or managed by intellectuals.

No doubt it was as much with this vision in their eyes as with the passion for justice toward others in their hearts that so many American writers, artists, and intellectuals joined the Communist party in the early 1930s, or at least lent it their moral support. (Conversely, it was the discovery by some, like the group associated with the magazine *Partisan Review,* that the Communists were contemptuous of aesthetic values and of any kind of intellectual independence that led them to break with the party and to invest their revolutionary hopes for a time in the anti-Stalinist Trotskyist movement.) My contention is that it was a similar vision of power—clearly seen by a few, only intuitively or unconsciously sensed by others—that brought about the radicalization and politicization of the intellectuals in the 1960s. What the prosperous young intellectuals who compared themselves to "niggers" were really "trying to tell us" was that they were being denied their "fair share," not of the middle-class security and comfort with which they were already so obviously and plentifully supplied, but of the political power which they believed should rightly be theirs. (Naturally, they never doubted for a moment that they would exercise it in the best interests of all, and especially the downtrodden.) This is why the issue of "participating in the decisions which affect our lives" became so important to the radicals of the sixties and later to their milder liberal progeny.

Within the radical New Left it was believed that power

would have to be wrested by force, and it was also believed—
sincerely believed—that this was possible because the United
States was in a "revolutionary situation." As in the depression, the failures of the system—its inability to eradicate
poverty and racism—were providing revolutionary fuel. But
now, in contrast to the depression, even the successes of the
system—the spread of affluence to the great majority of the
populace—were creating radical discontent. The "best" of
the young were refusing to join the "establishment"; they
were dropping out and developing a "counterculture" of
their own based on the rejection of the "Puritan ethic" and
indeed of all middle-class values: work, ambition, discipline,
monogamy, and the family. Clearly, then, the system was
no longer viable; clearly it was being destroyed by "internal
contradictions" which, if not precisely those foreseen by
Marx (for the working class was being subjected to em-
bourgeoisement rather than pauperization and could therefore no longer be depended upon to serve as the vanguard
of the revolution), were nevertheless deep enough to tear
everything apart and bring the entire structure down.

This analysis was developed long before American combat
troops were sent to Vietnam and long before the first riot
broke out in the black ghettos of the North. But it obviously
gained in credibility as the war became a more and more
burning issue, especially on the campuses, and as the civil-
rights movement, with its tactics of litigation and nonvio-
lence, gave way to a "Black Power" movement based on
violence and threats of violence. For with every collapse of
the authorities in the face of an aggressive challenge—violent
demonstrations, the seizure and occupation of buildings,
"nonnegotiable demands"—more and more evidence was
provided for the idea that the system was falling apart and
that a revolution was about to break out.

The sixties ended, however, not with a revolution but with

the election of Richard Nixon: Richard Nixon, who better than any single figure in American public life seemed to epitomize everything in opposition to which the adversary culture had always defined itself. But the response to this defeat was not a new withdrawal. It was, on the contrary, a new determination to mount an effective political challenge, this time "working within the system" to get rid of the usurper who had seized the throne and to place political power at long last into the proper hands. This effort, which called itself the New Politics, sought to forge a coalition of two disparate elements: those who were, or felt themselves to be, deprived of the full benefits of middle-class comfort and security (the blacks and the poor) and those who were, or felt themselves to be, deprived of the full benefits of political power (the New Class). Operating through the candidacy of George McGovern for President, the New Politics came infinitely closer to actual power than any political movement associated with the adversary culture had ever done before, and though it suffered a humiliating defeat at the hands of Richard Nixon in 1972, it participated centrally in the successful campaign to drive him from the White House in 1974. Two years later, the presidential candidate backed by the New Politics, Morris Udall, lost out to an ambiguous figure named Jimmy Carter who then went on as President to staff his administration with veterans of the New Politics and more recent converts to its point of view. Full political power, then, had not been achieved, but obviously great progress had been made.

Yet, so far as the adversary culture in particular was concerned, much greater progress had been made in the world of ideas and attitudes than in the political realm. By the end of the 1960s the values of the business class were no longer dominant in America—or even, it sometimes seemed from the readiness with which it assented to attacks on its own position, within the business class itself. In one sense, for example, individualism had grown rampant in America, but not at all in the sense once prized by the business world. The ascendant ethic preached in the public schools, in the mass media, and even in comic books and pornographic magazines now seemed to be that nothing—not wives, not husbands, not children, and certainly not the state—must stand in the way of the individual's right to self-fulfillment and self-expression in the realm of morals, sex, and personal relations (which was, of course, the adversary culture's traditional version of individualism as well as its answer to middle-class or bourgeois values). But where economic enterprise was concerned, the opposite view prevailed: there every obstacle must be put in the way of "rugged individualism" and the more state control the better. And a similar fate had overtaken the old materialism of the business class. Profits were now "obscene"; economic growth was now a "threat to the environment"; prosperity was now "waste" and the criminal squandering of putatively scarce natural resources.

Obviously, the progress of the adversary culture in the war of ideas served the political interests of the New Class. For the more the economic life of the country shifted from private to state-controlled enterprise, the less power would accrue to businessmen and the more power would accrue to the professional and technical intelligentsia. But toward the end of the 1960s, a new and complicating element began to enter the picture. Repelled by the sight that the sixties had vouchsafed of what the adversary culture looked like in action, and therefore of what it might look like in power, a group of dissident intellectuals, mostly, but not exclusively, associated with magazines like *Commentary* and the *Public Interest,* appeared on the scene to defend middle-class values, and even capitalism itself, as the indispensable basis of liberty, democracy, widespread material prosperity, and a whole range of private human decencies. One member of the group, Hilton Kramer, harking back to Joseph Schumpeter (who influenced other members of the group as well), even argued that the adversary culture itself owed its existence to these values, both in the sense that they had provided it with the freedom to develop—a freedom the "socialist" countries had never been willing to grant—and in the deeper sense that its commitment to experimentation and novelty was a reflection in aesthetic terms of the general bourgeois commitment to constant technological innovation and continuous social change.

These intellectual adversaries of the adversary culture were often called "neoconservatives," a designation happily accepted by some (like Irving Kristol) but rejected at first by most others, who continued to think of themselves as liberals. "Neoliberal" would perhaps have been a more accurate label for the entire group than neoconservative, but this label was destined to be claimed a little later by a different group of dissident liberals (themselves influenced by the neoconservatives).* In any case, the liberalism of the neoconservatives was old and not new—that is, it derived from the New Deal and not from the New Politics. The New Politics liberalism of the sixties and seventies, in the judgment of the neoconservatives, was not entitled to be called liberal at all, and was indeed antiliberal in many crucial respects. Thus, for example, the new "liberals," in direct violation of traditional liberal principles, supported quota systems rather than individual merit—or equality of result rather than equality of opportunity—as the road to social justice. But this brand of egalitarianism was not sim-

---

* If, as Kristol has said, a neoconservative is a "liberal who has been mugged by reality," a neoliberal, according to John Podhoretz, is a "liberal who has been mugged by a neoconservative."

ply antiliberal; it also contributed to the undermining of middle-class values by making rewards contingent upon membership in a group favored for one reason or another by the government, rather than upon individual effort and achievement. It could be understood, then, as an extension into concrete social policy of the adversary culture's assault on the "Protestant ethic."*

In thus challenging the adversary culture, the neoconservative dissidents did not go quite so far as William F. Buckley, Jr., on their Right, who once said that he would rather be ruled by the first two thousand names in the Boston telephone book than by the combined faculties of Harvard and MIT. But the neoconservatives (several of whom were themselves distinguished Harvard professors) went far enough in expressing doubt over the desirability of a society ruled by their own kind to suggest the possibility of a deepening schism within the intellectual community.

Certainly these intellectual adversaries of the adversary culture were exerting a marked influence by the mid-1970s. Their writings were being read and discussed in many circles, and the election of Ronald Reagan in 1980 could be, and was, seen as a mark of their spreading influence.

To be sure, they still represented a minority within the intellectual community, but no smaller perhaps than the adversary culture itself had once been within the world out of which it had dialectically emerged exactly a hundred years before. The effect the neoconservative dissidents might

---

* Of course there was a conflict between radical egalitarianism and the idea of a society run by intellectuals. But destroying middle-class values was more important for the moment than worrying about how the values that would replace them could be squared with those in the name of which the revolution was being fought. Needless to say, the New Class was not the first insurgent class in history to have faced this problem, and if its dreams of political rule were ever to come true, it would no doubt resolve the contradiction in the manner of all past revolutionaries: through ideological fiat backed by the coercive power of the state.

have on the future course of events was difficult to predict. But as the first century of business domination in America drew to a close, the very existence of a significant party of intellectuals to whom the defense of middle-class values seemed necessary to the preservation of liberty, democracy, and even civilization itself was already casting an anxious shadow over the otherwise cheerful prospects of the adversary culture in the realm of ideas and attitudes, and of the New Class in the arena of economic and political power.

PART THREE

East and West

7.

KISSINGER RECONSIDERED

Reading *Years of Upheaval*, the second volume of Henry Kissinger's memoirs, was for me a less overwhelming experience than reading its immediate predecessor, *White House Years*. But that was only because my astonishment at what Kissinger was capable of as a writer had already worn off by the time I had finished *White House Years* itself.

Kissinger in his disarming fashion likes to quote the reviewer of one of his early scholarly works who (allegedly) said: "I don't know if Dr. Kissinger is a great writer, but anyone who gets through this book is certainly a great reader." If the remark was ever in fact made, it was an exaggeration. Kissinger as a professor wrote in a serviceable academic style, which was no worse than the prose of most of his colleagues in the fields of political science and international affairs. On the other hand, he was certainly not as

lively or as lucid a stylist as certain of his academic colleagues. Be that as it may, if memory serves, there was little
if anything of a literary nature in his earlier work to prepare
us for *White House Years.* We did, however, have *White
House Years* to prepare us for *Years of Upheaval* which,
although self-contained in the sense of being entirely intelligible on its own, is really a continuation (though not yet
the completion) of the same book. When in due course the
third and final volume comes out, we will have a single unit
running to some four thousand densely printed pages. And
it will be—it already is—one of the great works of our time.

I use the word "great" both reluctantly and advisedly:
reluctantly, because I do not wish to contribute to the in-
flationary tendencies which have debauched the language
of literary criticism as surely as they have the currency of
monetary exchange; but advisedly, because in this case the
epithet for once designates the true value being claimed.

There is also another reason to insist on the word great
here, and that is the failure of so many who have written
about these memoirs to give them their proper due. It is one
thing to quarrel with Kissinger about his ideas and his
policies; I will be doing just that myself. But it is quite
another matter when no awareness is shown of the high
intellectual distinction with which those ideas are explicated
and the policies defended. And it is altogether scandalous
when people who presumably care about books as much
as they do about politics are unable to recognize or unwilling to acclaim a masterwork when they see one because
they are blinded or moved by political bias. Yet with an
occasional, and surprising, exception like Christopher Leh-
mann-Haupt and Stanley Hoffmann, the reviewers, first of
White House Years and now of *Years of Upheaval,* have
either been unremittingly hostile or grudging in their
acknowledgment of what Kissinger has done here.

Admittedly the length of these volumes is a problem, if only because they demand more time than most of us nowadays are willing to give to a book. Yet as an editor who has been known to cut a manuscript now and again and to judge the briefer version an improvement, I would have found it very difficult to shorten either *White House Years* or *Years of Upheaval* without sacrificing something good. It is true that in order to make *Years of Upheaval* self-contained, Kissinger goes over a certain amount of territory already traversed in *White House Years*. But aside from such patches of repetition, these volumes are astonishingly free of either padding or gratuitous detail. One might well say of them what Dr. Johnson said of *Paradise Lost,* that "none ever wished it longer than it is," while at the same time recognizing that they are not too long for what they deliver.

This does not mean that every page is equally interesting. So much ground is covered, so many subjects are explored in such rich and sometimes technical detail, that inevitably every reader will come upon sections that seem arid or dull. But even those sections (for example, discussions of the debate over SALT, or some of the minute-by-minute accounts of Kissinger's negotiations with foreign governments) are necessary to the historical record. Moreover, they always reward careful attention and often turn out to be as fascinating as they appear forbidding. Indeed, not the least stunning of Kissinger's talents as a writer is his ability to do justice to the technical complexities of a subject like arms control while making those complexities clear to any lay reader who is willing to slow down a bit and invest a little extra intellectual effort.

The paradox is that Kissinger unwittingly discourages the reader from exerting himself on such occasions by making it so easy for him the rest of the time. Hard as it is to pick these volumes up (in addition to being so long and looking so forbidding, they weigh about five pounds each), it is harder still to put them down. A reader who approaches them as a duty will invariably be rewarded with a pleasure: a wonderful story told wonderfully well.

It is not, however, as might have been expected, the story of Kissinger's spectacular career. There is almost nothing of a personal nature here. From time to time he refers to his origins as a Jewish refugee from Germany, or his years as a Harvard professor and as an adviser to Nelson Rockefeller. He tells us too how he happened to be hired by Richard Nixon in 1968 as National Security Adviser, and he explains why Nixon later decided to appoint him Secretary of State. But whereas Kissinger provides dozens of character sketches throughout these two volumes, the best of them breathtaking in their evocative power, and the least of them shrewd in their psychological insight, he shows no such gift for self-portraiture and no inclination toward the introspective. On the evidence of these memoirs, one would have to conclude that this man—who has become legendary for his arrogance and egomania—is, if anything, abnormally deficient in curiosity about himself. His interest in everyone and everything else in the world, by contrast, seems inexhaustible.

To convey some idea of how this combination of qualities works to control and color Kissinger's narrative style, let me take as a random example the account in *Years of Upheaval* of his first visit to Saudi Arabia in 1973, only two weeks after the oil embargo had been declared.

He begins here, as always, by setting the political context— in this instance Nixon's desperate desire to get the embargo lifted, not only for its own sake, but in order to demonstrate his mastery of foreign policy and hence buttress "his claim to continue in office" just at the point when "Watergate was winding its inexorable way through congressional and judicial procedures." Having spelled out the domestic political forces that influenced the workings of the episode, Kissinger then goes on to place it in its local setting by means of an analysis of Saudi Arabia in which history, geography, religion, and national psychology are interwoven and interrelated in a tour de force of compression and lucidity. Then comes a typical humorous description of his reception, accompanied by a disquisition on the cultural implications of the physical and architectural surroundings which are themselves presented with a vividness beyond the literary powers of a good many contemporary novelists:

> Faisal's palace was on a monumental scale. Preceded by two sword carriers, I was taken to a tremendous hall that seemed as large as a football field. Dozens of the distinguished men of the Kingdom (women, of course, being strictly segregated) in identical black robes and white headdresses were seated along the walls, immobile and silent. There was incense in the air, circulated by the air conditioning. What seemed like a hundred yards away on a slightly raised pedestal sat King Faisal ibn Abd al-Aziz Al Sa'ud, aquiline of feature, regal of bearing. He rose as I entered, forcing all the princes and sheiks to follow suit in a flowing balletlike movement of black and white. He took one step toward me: I had to traverse the rest of the way. I learned later that his taking a step forward was a sign of great courtesy. At the time, I was above all conscious of the seeming eternity it took to reach the pedestal.

In one respect, this passage is untypical, since it leads straight into a rare reference to Kissinger's personal background ("His Majesty and I sat side by side for a few minutes overlooking the splendid assemblage while I reflected in some wonder what strange twists of fate had caused a refugee from Nazi persecution to wind up in Arabia as the representative of American democracy"). But we soon discover, what we might already have suspected, that the reference is not a gratuitous touch. It is there because it is essential to a full appreciation of the outlandish aspect of Kissinger's encounter with Faisal, who proceeds to tell him that

> Jews and Communists were working now in parallel, now together, to undermine the civilized world as we knew it. Oblivious to my ancestry—or delicately putting me into a special category—Faisal insisted that an end had to be put once and for all to the dual conspiracy of Jews and Communists. The Middle East outpost of that plot was the State of Israel, put there by Bolshevism for the principal purpose of dividing America from the Arabs.

Kissinger's comment on this outburst—the smile playing over the prose, the wit, the wry self-deprecation both concealing and revealing enormous self-confidence—is characteristic of the way he talks about himself throughout these memoirs:

> It was hard to know where to begin in answering such a line of reasoning. When Faisal went on to argue that the Jewish-Communist conspiracy was now trying to take over the American government, I decided the time had come to change the subject. I did so by asking His Majesty about a picture on the far wall, which I took to be a decorative work of art. It was a holy oasis, I was informed—representational art being forbidden in Islam. This faux pas threw Faisal into some minutes of deep melancholy, causing conversation around the table to stop altogether. In the unearthly silence my colleagues must have wondered what I had done so quickly to impair the West's oil supplies. I did not help matters by referring to Sadat as the leader of the Arabs. His Majesty's morose reaction showed that there was a limit beyond which claims to Arab solidarity could not be pushed.

After a few more amusing details about the way this weird conversation was conducted, Kissinger, modulating smoothly into a serious key, composes a little essay on the mind and character of King Faisal so thoroughly informed by sympathetic imagination that it even manages to make a kind of sense out of the speech on Communism and Zionism:

> However bizarre it sounded to Western visitors, [Faisal's speech] was clearly deeply felt. At the same time it reflected precisely the tactical necessities of the Kingdom. The strident anti-Communism helped reassure America and established a claim on protection against outside threats. . . . The virulent opposition to Zionism reassured radicals and the PLO and thus reduced their incentive to follow any temptation to undermine the monarchy domestically. And its thrust was vague enough to imply no precise consequences: it dictated few policy options save a general anti-Communism.

The section on this visit to Riyadh then moves toward its conclusion with a meticulous account of the negotiating sessions between Faisal and Kissinger, which, like the dozens of other such accounts scattered throughout these memoirs, gives a superlative picture of how diplomacy is actually conducted.

What we have here is writing of the very highest order. It is writing that is equally at ease in portraiture and abstract analysis; that can shape a narrative as skillfully as it can paint a scene; that can achieve marvels of compression while moving at an expansive and leisurely pace. It is writing that can shift without strain or falsity of tone from the *gravitas* befitting a book about great historical events to the humor and irony dictated by an unfailing sense of human proportion.

Kissinger the writer, then, has established a secure claim

to greatness. But that is not the claim he is staking in these memoirs. What he wants, above all, is to explain and defend his achievements as a diplomat or (to use the word he himself generally prefers) a statesman. On this point too his memoirs are a surprise. For what they reveal is that if Kissinger did achieve greatness in this area, it was as a practitioner of the art of diplomacy and not as the "conceptualizer" he was always praised for being.

The reason this is surprising, of course, is that he was, after all, an intellectual rather than a professional diplomat. He had studied and taught and written about international affairs, but when he became Nixon's chief adviser on foreign policy in 1968 he had had very little practical experience in diplomacy or the conduct of high-level negotiations. During the Kennedy and Johnson administrations he had done a certain amount of consulting and he had participated on a relatively low level in one or two diplomatic missions. But that, so far as we can tell from the memoirs, was all.

Of McGeorge Bundy, who blazed the trail Kissinger was to follow from Harvard to the post of National Security Adviser, Arthur Schlesinger, Jr., could say with typical Cambridge smugness: "I had seen him learn how to dominate the faculty of Harvard University, a throng of intelligent and temperamental men; after that training, one could hardly doubt his capacity to deal with Washington bureaucrats." But unlike Bundy, who had been a dean, Kissinger had only been a professor. Hence he had not even had a chance to learn the game of power in the interdepartmental conflicts of the academic jungle before graduating into the real jungles of international conflict where the stakes are so much higher and the talents required to play are of an entirely different order.

Because Kissinger is so incurious—or perhaps only reticent—about himself, we learn nothing from these memoirs that would help us understand how this intellectual, this professor, with no practical diplomatic experience to speak of, could with perfect assurance and a poise that would normally require many years of training to develop, leap overnight and in one bound into the topmost reaches of international statesmanship. There is nothing here to explain how this naturalized American, still speaking with a heavy German accent and (presumably) still carrying the burdens of uncertainty and inner doubt that afflict all refugees and to which even native-born American Jews of Kissinger's generation have so often been prey, could, again overnight, begin dealing on equal terms with all the major figures of the age.

As in the passage quoted above about his first meeting with King Faisal of Saudi Arabia, Kissinger is fond of poking gentle fun at himself for the gaucheries and faux pas he always seems to be committing on his breathless and bewildering diplomatic rounds from one country to another, each with its own manners and mores and hence with its own innumerable opportunities for getting things wrong. In one place he talks out of turn; in another he fails to follow the right procedure in reviewing the troops who have come to honor him; in a third he elicits a pained response for his American obtuseness in missing a subtle signal during the course of a negotiation. But it goes without saying that this easy willingness to tell funny stories at his own expense is the surest mark of a supreme self-confidence.

And indeed, far from being thrown by the requirements of his job as the official envoy of the United States of America and the main shaper of its relations with the rest of the world, he demonstrates a mastery that is all but incredible. In the same month, or the same week, or even on the same day, he will turn his attention to the technicalities of the SALT negotiations, the intricacies of the Arab-

Israeli conflict, the problems of the Atlantic Alliance, and the niceties of the developing relation with China. When he is traveling, especially during the "shuttle diplomacy" that he conducted after the Yom Kippur war between Israel and Egypt, and then Israel and Syria, he maintains an alert sense of the issues and the personalities he is dealing with, while simultaneously supervising all the other business of his office.

Sleepless, racked by jet lag, assailed by a multitude of crises, he never seems to tire to the point of losing his edge or growing impatient with the nuances that are—so he repeatedly tells us—the lifeblood of diplomacy. He always seems to know where he is, he always seems to keep a fascinated and wary eye on his interlocutor, he is rarely at a loss for the humorous quip or the soothing remark or the daring proposal when an opening suddenly presents itself. When he meets with someone like Mao Zedong, whom he regards as a titanic historical figure, he can be awed without being over-awed. But he is equally capable of taking the proper measure of a lesser personage like Assad of Syria without the condescension that is the surest path to stupidity in a diplomat. A believer in the centrality of power, he nevertheless has a judicious respect for even the least powerful of nations and the sensitivity of an anthropologist to the distinctive features and beauties of even the least imposing of cultures. No wonder he won the answering admiration and affection of so many of the leaders he dealt with, including many who counted themselves enemies of the United States.

If Kissinger ever suffered any anxiety in becoming National Security Adviser and then Secretary of State, or in performing the duties of those offices, it is not recorded in these memoirs. Being (as he would perhaps be willing to admit) human, he cannot be an absolute stranger to anxiety.

But as a statesman he was at ease only as a man could be who had found the job that he was clearly born to do.

In this respect, the contrast between Kissinger and Nixon could not have been sharper or more poignant. In one of the most extraordinary passages of these memoirs—it comes toward the end of *Years of Upheaval*—Kissinger describes an automobile trip he took with Nixon and his friend Bebe Rebozo in California during the summer of 1970. What Nixon wanted was to show Kissinger and Rebozo the house where he was born and the town in which he grew up. After pointing out various landmarks of his childhood and his youth, "Nixon suddenly conceived the idea that Rebozo and I should see not only his origin but how far he had come." Accordingly he directed his driver to the place he had lived for two years after losing the presidential election of 1960 and where he had regained his sense of balance. But astonishingly, he was unable to locate it. Thus the President of the United States and his National Security Adviser spent well over an hour searching "every canyon and the streets leading off them" in the vicinity of the Beverly Hills Hotel, without ever finding the house they were looking for.

Rightly seeing in this episode an allegory of Nixon's life, Kissinger comments: "He was at ease with his youth; he could recount his struggles; he could not find the locus of his achievements. . . . On his way to success he had traveled on many roads, but he had found no place to stand, no haven, no solace, no inner peace. He never learned where his home was."

Henry Kissinger had traveled on many roads, too, but unlike Nixon he did find a home. Quoting Archimedes ("Give me a place to stand and I shall move the earth"), Kissinger remarks that "Nixon sought to move the world but he lacked a firm foothold." Yet Kissinger obviously discovered a firm foothold in the very place that failed to provide one for the poor boy from Whittier who had put him there. Even in the White House Richard Nixon, the man who "lacked a firm foothold," remained "slightly out of focus." For he "had set himself a goal beyond human capacity: to make himself over entirely; to create a new personality as if alone of all mankind he could overcome his destiny." Not Kissinger. Though he does not say so himself, but as we know from the simple fact that this enormously ambitious man trying to make his way in circles not particularly hospitable to foreigners never even bothered to get rid of his accent, Kissinger was guilty of no such "presumption." Therefore he did not pay "the fearful price" he believes the gods exacted of Nixon: "the price of congenital insecurity." And thus it was that the refugee from Fürth, Germany, unlike the refugee from Whittier, California, found a home in Washington, and a firm foothold, and the sharpest possible focus for his talents and his energies, which then proceeded to pour forth in prodigious torrents of virtuoso activity.

Whether he moved the earth is, however, another question. What he attempted to do, always working with and often (it is important to remember) under the direction of Nixon, was to build a new "structure of peace" in the world. This involved, first, arranging for an "honorable" American withdrawal from Vietnam; second, establishing a new relationship with the Soviet Union to be known as détente and to be based on negotiation rather than confrontation; and third, inaugurating an American relationship with Communist China. All this was to be accomplished, moreover, within the context of a diminishing American presence in the world. Indeed, it was precisely because domestic support for American intervention abroad had been eroded by Vietnam that substitutes had to be found to prevent the balance of power, on which Kissinger and Nixon believed that peace depended, from tilting dangerously toward the Soviet Union.

In presiding over what was in effect a strategic retreat, Nixon and Kissinger were trying to make certain above all else that the retreat would not turn—as retreats are always in danger of doing—into a wholesale rout. This consideration in itself precluded a precipitous withdrawal from Vietnam. We had to leave in such a way as to give South Vietnam a fighting chance to save itself from conquest by the Communist North, thus vindicating the purpose of our own intervention and demonstrating the reliability of American commitments.

At the same time, we had to find a way to restrain Soviet expansionism that did not depend entirely or even largely on the use or the threatened use of American military power. This new strategy, as Nixon and Kissinger conceived it, was composed of two tactical strands. The first and more important was to offer incentives (mainly consisting of economic benefits) for Soviet moderation and restraint, and to threaten penalties (mainly consisting of the withdrawal of those benefits) for aggressive or adventurist activity. This, in essence, was what détente meant. Although the rhetoric in which Nixon and Kissinger and their supporters talked about it was usually more grandiose, détente was at bottom an effort to compensate for the loss of American military power (the will to use it as well as the relative edge in hardware) with a more purposeful deployment of economic power. In this scheme, the function of arms control was to keep the military balance stable, both for its own sake and because reducing the influence of the military factor would make the economic factor more effective.

The second tactical strand of the new strategy for containing the Soviet Union at a time of diminishing American power and will was the so-called Nixon Doctrine. This en-

tailed finding regional allies or surrogates who would as-
sume the responsibility for deterring Soviet expansionist
moves and, if necessary, resisting them by force. The United
States would supply arms for this purpose, but such regional
surrogates as Iran under the Shah would do the rest. The
opening to China, whatever else it may have been intended
to accomplish—and there were undoubtedly many reasons
for the move—has to be understood in the first instance as
a product of the Nixon Doctrine. For China too was to be
built up as yet another restraint on Soviet expansionism. No
one, certainly not Kissinger, was so foolish as to think of
the Chinese as an American surrogate. But playing the
China card was undoubtedly part of the overall strategy of
finding substitutes for the formerly all but exclusive reliance
on American military power to contain the Soviet Union in
Asia and indeed everywhere else in the world.

It was, no doubt about it, a brilliant strategic conception,
each element consistent with every other and all together
blending into an organic whole. That it corresponded with
Nixon's instincts and impulses we can be certain, and there
is no way of knowing where exactly, in the collaboration
between them, Nixon left off and Kissinger began. In general (so Kissinger tells us) Nixon, in effect, saw what had
to be done and gave the orders to do it; the details of the
execution were left to others—and where foreign policy was
concerned, others meant Henry Kissinger.

This is not to suggest that the strategy was all Nixon and
the tactics all Kissinger. For it was Kissinger who, at first
under the pseudonym "a high official" and later openly in
his own voice, took over the job of explaining and articulat-
ing the administration's policy—in press briefings, in interviews with influential columnists like James Reston, and in
private conversations both with journalists and with con-
gressmen. Thus the exquisite balance and symmetry in the

design of the overall strategy must surely have owed at least as much, and more, to Kissinger the intellectual, the "conceptualizer," as to Nixon the politician.

Whatever the share of responsibility—credit *or* blame—to be assigned to Kissinger, however, one might say of this strategy what Edmund Burke said of Lord North's treatment of the American colonies: "This fine-spun scheme had the usual fate of all exquisite policy." Brilliant though it was in achieving perfect internal coherence, it failed because it misjudged the nature of the Soviet threat on the one side and the nature of American public opinion on the other.

That men like Kissinger and Nixon should have misjudged the nature of the Soviet threat is on the face of it hard to believe. Neither one of them was in the least subject to sentimental illusions about the Soviet Union; neither had any sympathy for the Soviets or any admiration for their leaders. Whereas Kissinger writes about Mao Zedong and Zhou Enlai with a respect bordering on and occasionally crossing over into reverence, he is sardonic about Brezhnev and Gromyko. Nor did Kissinger or Nixon ever doubt that the Soviet Union had expansionist aims or that it was capable of great ruthlessness in the pursuit of those aims.

At the same time, however, while Kissinger here, and Nixon in his own writings, always make their obeisances to the role of ideology in determining Soviet behavior on the international scene, for the most part they saw the Soviet Union as a nation-state like any other, motivated by the same range of interests that define and shape the foreign policies of all nation-states. From this perspective—the perspective of *Realpolitik*—Communist Russia was not all that different from Czarist Russia, the facts of geography, history, and ancestral culture being far more decisive than the ideas of Marx and Lenin.

If this were indeed the case, it would certainly be possible to make a deal of the kind contemplated by the policy of détente. If, in other words, the aims of the Soviet Union were limited, they could be respected and even to a certain extent satisfied through negotiation and compromise, with the resultant settlement policed by means other than, and short of, actual military force.

But what if the Soviet Union is not a "normal" nation-state? What if in this case ideology overrides interest in the traditional sense? What if Soviet aims are unlimited? In short (and to bring up the by-now familiar contending comparisons), what if the Soviet Union bears a closer resemblance to the Germany of Hitler than to the Germany of Kaiser Wilhelm? Wilhelmine Germany was an expansionist power seeking a place in the imperial sun and nothing more than that. Hitler, by contrast, was a revolutionary seeking to overturn the going international system and to replace it with a new order dominated by Germany (which also meant the political culture of Nazism). For tactical reasons and in order to mislead, Hitler sometimes pretended that all he wanted was the satisfaction of specific grievances, and those who were taken in by this pretense not unreasonably thought they could "do business" with him. But there was no way of doing business—that is, negotiating a peaceful settlement—with Hitler. As a revolutionary with unlimited aims, he offered only two choices: resistance or submission.

All the evidence suggests that the Soviet Union poses the same kind of threat, and the same narrow range of choices, to the West. It has committed itself by word and deed to the creation of a "socialist" world. There is no reason to think that it can be talked out of this commitment or even (as, at bottom, détente assumes) bribed out of it. It may well be, as we are often told, that the Soviet leaders no longer believe subjectively in Communism. But whatever they say to themselves in the privacy of their own minds, they are (to borrow from their own vocabulary) *objectively* the prisoners of Marxian and Leninist doctrines. Without these doctrines, which mandate steady international advances in the cause of "socialism," they have no way to legitimize their monopoly of power within the Soviet Union itself. Hence, even if they wanted to limit their aims and become a "status-quo power," they would be unable to do so without committing political suicide.

What this means is that the conflict between the Soviet Union and the West is not subject to resolution by the traditional tools of diplomacy. Or, to put the point another way, given the nature of the Soviet threat, détente is not possible. Certain agreements may be possible from time to time, but they will invariably cover ground (cultural exchanges, arrangements for travel and communications, and the like) that is peripheral or even trivial from the point of view of the central issue. Where really important ground is touched upon, the agreement will invariably result in a Soviet advantage.

This is not because the Soviets are necessarily better at negotiating than we are or because they will necessarily cheat. They may or may not be better and they may or may not cheat. It is, rather, because in any negotiation between a party with limited aims and a party with unlimited aims, the party with limited aims is bound to lose in the very nature of things. Even a deal that on the surface promises mutual benefits will work out to the advantage of the side pursuing a strategy of victory over the side pursuing a strategy of accommodation and peace.

Thus, for example—as Kissinger himself has had the honesty and the courage to admit—the expanded commercial relations that were supposed to encourage Soviet restraint did not prevent the invasion of Afghanistan or the repression of Solidarity in Poland (not to mention such earlier Soviet moves as the dispatch of Cuban proxies to Angola). But economic "linkages" did work to restrain the American response on each of these occasions and to paralyze the Europeans altogether.

The case of arms control is perhaps less obvious but it is no less telling. What have the SALT negotiations accomplished? SALT I, which Kissinger defends with his customary brilliance (but with uncustomary heat), may well have been the best agreement possible at the time. Nevertheless, whereas it did nothing to limit the buildup of Soviet strategic arms, it did contribute to the slowing down of the American buildup.

Again, this was not because the Soviets cheated (though they may have, just as a roulette wheel may be fixed though the house wins even when it is honest). It was because, as the history of disarmament agreements in this century should have taught everyone, such agreements result in disarming only the party that wants to disarm and not the party that has no intention of doing so. That is what happened after the naval agreements of the twenties and thirties, when the United States, the British, and the French did not even build up to their legal limits while the Japanese and then the Germans not only did so but invented ways of exceeding their quotas while remaining within the letter of the law. And it is exactly what happened after SALT I, a period in which the Soviet buildup continued on its relentless course in both quantity and quality while the United States was either standing still or actually cutting back.

Kissinger frequently argues that a tough policy toward the Soviet Union can only enlist the support of public opinion in the United States (and in the West generally) if it is accompanied by a strategy for peace. People, that is, must be convinced that their leaders are doing everything possible to resolve the conflict by peaceful means before they will vote for the increases in defense spending, and before they will back the firm stands against Soviet expansionism that Kissinger himself has consistently favored as the indispensable foundation of American influence and as a necessary element even of a successful policy of détente.

But the historical record suggests the opposite. In relation first to Nazi Germany and then to Soviet Russia, Western public opinion was lulled by negotiated agreements and was only galvanized at those moments when the nature of the enemy revealed itself unambiguously in action.

Where Hitler was concerned, for example, it was not until the invasion of Poland that the British public finally awoke from the dream of Munich—that great monument to the illusion that Nazi Germany was a state like any other with limited and hence negotiable ambitions. In the case of the Soviet Union, this illusion comes and goes. It was blasted for the first time after the Czechoslovak coup of 1948, only to rise again during the period of de-Stalinization of the fifties until it was blasted by the invasion of Hungary, only to rise again during the "thaw" of the sixties until it was blasted by the invasion of Czechoslovakia, only to rise again in the time of détente until it was blasted by the invasion of Afghanistan.

The trouble is that each time the illusion returns, it seems to grow stronger, fed by fear as the Soviet military arsenal also grows stronger. Now that it is rising again, it is indeed stronger than ever, forming the basis of the most explosive outburst of unilateralist sentiment yet to erupt in Western Europe, and of an antinuclear hysteria in the United States that is well on its way to becoming a more respectable cover for isolationism than any of the other disguises isolationism has recently assumed.

The misreading of the nature of American public opinion

that underlay détente was thus symbiotically connected to the misreading of the nature of the Soviet Union itself. The American people for better or worse have always been and still are very reluctant to support large standing armies, let alone to use them in combat, merely for geopolitical reasons. In the absence of some higher meaning, the idealistic Wilsonian strain in the American character is likely to be overwhelmed by the ever-present isolationist temptation. Therefore, as I once put it, "by representing the Soviet Union as a competing superpower with whom we could negotiate peaceful and stable accommodations—instead of a Communist state hostile in its very nature to us and trying to extend its rule and its political culture over a wider and wider area of the world—the Nixon, Ford, and Carter administrations robbed the Soviet-American conflict of the moral and political dimensions for the sake of which sacrifices could be intelligibly demanded by the government and willingly made by the people."

In *Years of Upheaval* Kissinger calls this "the subtlest critique" of détente, but the generosity of his characterization does not imply agreement. "The argument that the American people cannot understand a complex challenge and a complex strategy to meet it," he writes, "that unable to handle both deterrence and coexistence it must base its policy on truculence, reflects a lack of faith in democracy."

Having so often been accused—though never by me—of lacking faith in democracy, Kissinger must have taken a special pleasure in thus turning the tables on some of his critics. But the issue here is not democracy; it is, rather, the nature of the American character. Kissinger, who is so good at delineating national character when he talks about other peoples, and whose mastery in practicing the art of diplomacy is so intimately tied to his respect for the limitations and possibilities flowing out of the national character of his opposite numbers, somehow refuses to see that the people of his own country, no less than the Chinese or the Israelis or the Vietnamese, are shaped by the facts of geography, history, religion, and culture and are therefore capable of certain things and not of others. He knows that it is foolish to demand of other nations what the facts of their situation make it impossible for them to give. But he seems not to know that this is equally true of the United States.

Given the nature of the American national character, a very high price had to be paid for the achievement of which Kissinger is perhaps most proud and for which the Nixon administration has been universally applauded—the opening to China. The strategic purpose of striking a de facto alliance with Communist China was to enlist its help in containing Soviet imperialism. But the question arose then, and continues to bedevil us today, of whether a China allied to the United States contributes any more to the containment of the Soviet Union than a China treated with benign neglect. After all, the number of Soviet divisions pinned down on the Chinese border before Kissinger went to Beijing has not increased.

On the other hand, by befriending one of the two great Communist colossi, we have made it harder to explain to ourselves what the struggle with the other is all about. In this way too the Soviet-American conflict has been robbed of the moral and political significance without which the dangers and the sacrifices it involves begin to seem pointless. People then begin to wonder why, if we can support Communist China, we should put ourselves at risk to resist Communist Russia. Why not let the Russians work their will in the Persian Gulf, or for that matter in Western Europe? Or, if the only objection to the establishment of

Communist regimes in countries like Nicaragua and El Salvador is that they are tied to the Soviet Union, why not woo them away?

Indeed, underlying much discussion of these matters in the United States nowadays is the idea, rarely made explicit, but present in the logic of particular proposals, that the safest course for us is to help sponsor a world of Communist regimes which are independent of the Soviet Union. Instead of making the world safe for democracy, we are urged to make it safe for Titoism.

To the extent that the opening to China was part of the Nixon Doctrine, then, one can say that this component of the new strategy—a strategy, to repeat, aimed at finding substitutes for American military power at a time when that power was in relative decline and when the will to serve as "policeman of the world" was declining even further— rested on the same misjudgment of the American national character as did the détente policy, which represented the other major component of the overall strategy.

Of course the Nixon Doctrine cannot yet be said to have failed the test of China. But it can most definitely be said to have failed the two other tests it has undergone. The first was in Vietnam, when, after the withdrawal of American troops, the United States Congress doomed the South Vietnamese to defeat at the hands of the Communist forces by cutting off military aid even in the midst of an invasion by the North Vietnamese army. The second was in Iran, when we either would not or could not (it makes no practical difference) save the government on which the Nixon Doctrine depended in that region from being overthrown by forces hostile to the United States.

When Vietnam was abandoned, Kissinger was still in office, but his protests and pleas fell on deaf congressional ears; by the time the Shah was abandoned, Kissinger was a private citizen, and his protests were *a fortiori* of no avail. He blames Watergate, but there are reasons to believe that even without Watergate American public opinion would have opposed continued involvement in Vietnam after the withdrawal of our troops.* The case of Iran is harder to judge, but even there one wonders whether American public opinion under any President (even a Nixon undamaged by Watergate) would have countenanced the bloodletting that would have been necessary to keep the Shah in power once the revolutionary mobs had hit the streets.

In short, as a "conceptualizer" Kissinger was very brilliant but for the most part wrong. The "structure of peace" he envisioned was an illusion, based on a misconception of what was possible in the real world. Since such misconceptions are common to intellectuals—who are always in danger of getting carried away by ideas—it is tempting to blame the intellectual in Kissinger for his errors as a statesman. But if he (rather than circumstances like Watergate) is to be blamed at all, it is paradoxically the diplomat rather than the intellectual in him at whom the accusing finger should be pointed.

Kissinger was so good at diplomacy, so great a virtuoso in the negotiating arts, that he may well have come to imagine that he could negotiate *anything;* and this may have led him into the mistake (which the intellectual in him could reinforce with dazzling rationalizations) of trying to negotiate the nonnegotiable. Throughout these volumes, whenever a stalemated negotiation is being described, the vision of the *breakthrough* shimmers in the distance, and when it comes, the sense of achievement is so great and so vividly conveyed that the reader not only shares in it but is in danger of joining Kissinger in forgetting for the moment

* I spell out these reasons in detail in chapter 4 of my book, *Why We Were in Vietnam.*

that in at least two major cases it ultimately turned out to be a mirage. The Paris accords that seemed to end the Vietnam War are one such case of a "breakthrough" in a conflict that could not be settled by compromise or accommodation; the 1972 agreement with the Soviet Union on the Basic Principles of Détente was another.

There is one more great conflict in the world, to which, as it happens, more space is devoted in *Years of Upheaval* than to any other: the Arab-Israeli conflict. Is it also non-negotiable? Certainly the essential feature of the nonnegotiable conflict is there. One side seeks victory, in this instance meaning not merely the conquest or the domination but the total destruction of the other side, which for its part seeks peaceful coexistence and accommodation. For many years the Arabs were entirely open about the unlimited character of their ambitions with respect to Israel. Nasser proclaimed that he wanted to drive the Jews of Israel into the sea, and the Arab world as a whole was united in the famous three "No's" proclaimed at Khartoum in 1967: No recognition, No negotiation, No peace. So long as this "rejectionist" position held, not even the most talented negotiator—not even Henry Kissinger—could see any chance of real motion toward a settlement. But with the rise of Sadat, and with his decision to inch his way toward a new and therefore potentially negotiable position, possibilities opened up that had not been there before; and at this point even a less perceptive diplomat than Henry Kissinger might have seen the faint glimmerings of a breakthrough at the end of a very long tunnel. Kissinger is frank to admit that he was a little slow in taking the full measure of Sadat, but once he did, there was no stopping him in pursuit of this most prized (because most elusive) breakthrough of all.

It was said at the time, and can still be maintained, that Egypt was egged on to attack Israel in 1973 by the Soviets (who thereby violated the provision in the Basic Principles of Détente calling on the two superpowers to exercise a restraining influence on third parties lest they themselves be drawn directly into the conflict). Kissinger, however, did not and does not see it that way. What he came to believe was that Sadat had launched the Yom Kippur War, not because of the Soviets, and not in order to destroy Israel, but to establish the psychological precondition for making peace with Israel: the restoration of Egyptian honor. This meant that Egypt must not be subjected to a humiliating military defeat. Thus while the United States was making certain through the supply of equipment that Israel would not be defeated by a Soviet-armed opponent, and while Nixon and Kissinger were deterring a direct Soviet intervention by putting U.S. forces on alert, their policy simultaneously required that Israel be denied a decisive victory.

The policy, in effect, was to contrive a virtual draw. This would leave Egypt feeling that its honor had been restored and would therefore make dealing with the Israelis psychologically possible; it would leave the Israelis indebted to the United States for saving them from being overwhelmed; it would therefore leave the United States (as Sadat often put it) with "99 percent of the cards," and would also result in a severe diminution of Soviet power in the Middle East. For an inconclusive end to the war would demonstrate that, while the United States would not permit the Arabs to win a military victory over Israel (the only kind of victory the Soviet connection could promise), only American diplomacy could help the Arabs recover territory that they had lost to the Israelis on the battlefield.

The outlines of this overall design were sufficiently clear even while the Yom Kippur War was still going on. They were discerned, for example, by such observers as Walter Laqueur and Edward N. Luttwak who, writing in collaboration, accused Kissinger of dragging his feet in resupplying the Israelis with vital military equipment in order to make the scheme work. Others, including Kissinger himself, blamed the second echelon of the Defense Department for this delay, and I must say that my original belief in the Laqueur-Luttwak interpretation has been shaken by his account of the episode in *Years of Upheaval*.

In any event, the Yom Kippur War *was* concluded in the way the new strategy required: in the end the Israelis were saved by a heroic American resupply effort; Egyptian honor was preserved by American pressure on Israel to spare the encircled Third Army; the Soviets were squeezed out of the ensuing diplomatic play; and the United States, in the person of Henry Kissinger, became the central actor in the Middle East. The military disengagement between Israel and Egypt that Kissinger negotiated in the course of the first example of "shuttle diplomacy" the world had ever seen led ultimately to the signing of a separate peace between the two parties: a stunning breakthrough indeed which, although not arranged directly by Kissinger himself (he was out of office by then), must be considered the direct progeny of his original achievement.

If the peace holds, Kissinger will have been vindicated; if, however, Egypt, having used American diplomacy to get what it could not win on the battlefield, should return (whether openly or covertly) to the rejectionist fold, another example will have been added to the Paris agreements on Vietnam of the terrible dangers of contriving a negotiated settlement between a party that wants peace and a party that, although it may at certain moments pretend otherwise, wants only victory.

Whatever happens, however, Kissinger is surely right in saying, as he often does, that the statesman works in darkness, that he is always forced to make choices, not only without foreknowledge of the future, but usually even without adequate knowledge of what is going on in the present. One salient virtue of these memoirs is the sense Kissinger gives us of how the process works from day to day, from hour to hour, sometimes even from minute to minute. We are drawn in, we share in the anxieties and excitements of one crisis after another, we are in suspense while we read, even though we know what the outcome will be.

For myself, even when following Kissinger through the execution of a policy with which I disagree, I find it very hard to fault or blame him. What else could he have done? What better could *anyone* have done? That is the feeling I get as I read, and it is undoubtedly the feeling he wants us all to get. Yet valuable as these memoirs are, they would have been more valuable still if Kissinger—having evoked the circumstances in which he did what he did and having convinced us that there was probably no better alternative available at the time—had added the dimension of hindsight and commented, from the perspective of today, on where and how he nevertheless went wrong.

On the evidence of some of his recent statements, for example, he has changed his mind about détente, or at least certain features of détente (such as the effects of economic linkage), and about arms control (whether there is such a thing as strategic superiority and what can be done with it). But so busy is he here with the effort to explain and justify his earlier views that he scarcely does more than hint at the revisions time and experience have wrought in his thinking. Understandable though this is, it remains a pity. For as the foreign policy of the Reagan administration has revealed, we will never recover from some of the illusions of the past until we arrive as a nation at a franker and more realistic assessment than Kissinger provides here.

For example, in defending himself against those (myself

included) who have pointed out that the fate of the Shah has demonstrated that the United States cannot safely rely on surrogates to defend its interests in the Persian Gulf, Kissinger asks what alternative there was to this policy at a time when neither Congress nor American public opinion would have sanctioned the stationing of American forces in the region. But the fact that there may have been no alternative under the circumstances prevailing at the time does not mean that the policy was sound. It may well have been the best we could do, but we now know that even the best turned out to be not good enough.

Perhaps it is too much to expect Kissinger himself, the most interested of all parties, to provide the disinterested critical assessment of the past we so desperately need. On the other hand, there is no one on the face of the earth from whom such a reassessment would come with greater authority.

In the meantime, and despite this deficiency, I think it is important, and especially for one like myself who was and remains opposed to the political strategy in whose defense these memoirs were written, to emphasize that they have already earned a place among the great books of their kind and among the great works of our time.

8.

AN OPEN LETTER TO
MILAN KUNDERA

Dear Milan Kundera:

Several years ago, a copy of the bound galleys of your novel, *The Book of Laughter and Forgetting,* came into my office for review. As a magazine editor I get so many books every week in that form that unless I have a special reason I rarely do more than glance at their titles. In the case of *The Book of Laughter and Forgetting* I had no such special reason. By 1980 your name should have been more familiar to me, but in fact I had only a vague impression of you as an East European dissident*—so vague that, I am now ashamed to confess, I could not have said for certain which country you came from: Hungary? Yugoslavia? Czechoslovakia? Perhaps even Poland?

---

* Since then you have taught me that the term East Europe is wrong because the countries in question belong to the West and that we should speak instead of Central Europe. But in 1980 I did not yet understand this.

Nor was I particularly curious about you either as an individual or as a member of the class of "East" European dissident writers. This was not because I was or am unsympathetic to dissidents in Communist regimes or those living in exile in the West. On the contrary, as a passionate anti-Communist, I am all too sympathetic—at least for their own good as writers.

"How many books about the horrors of life under Communism am I supposed to read? How many ought I to read?" asks William F. Buckley, Jr., another member of the radically diminished fraternity of unregenerate anti-Communists in the American intellectual world. Like Buckley, I felt that there were a good many people who still needed to learn about "the horrors of life under Communism," but that I was not one of them. Pleased though I was to see books by dissidents from behind the Iron Curtain published and disseminated, I resisted reading any more of them myself.

What then induced me to begin reading *The Book of Laughter and Forgetting?* I have no idea. Knowing your work as well as I do now, I can almost visualize myself as a character in a Kundera novel, standing in front of the cabinet in my office where review copies of new books are kept, suddenly being seized by one of them while you, the author, break into the picture to search speculatively for the cause. But whatever answer you might come up with, I have none. I simply do not know why I should have been drawn against so much resistance to *The Book of Laughter and Forgetting.* What I do know is that once I had begun reading it, I was transfixed.

Twenty-five years ago, as a young literary critic, I was sent an advance copy of a book of poems called *Life Studies.* It was by Robert Lowell, a poet already famous and much honored in America, but whose earlier work had generally left me cold. I therefore opened *Life Studies* with no great expectation of pleasure, but what I found there was more than pleasure. Reading it, I told Lowell in a note thanking him for the book, made me remember, as no other new volume of verse had for a long time, why I had become interested in poetry in the first place. That is exactly what *The Book of Laughter and Forgetting* did for my old love of the novel—a love grown cold and stale and dutiful.

During my years as a literary critic, I specialized in contemporary fiction, and one of the reasons I eventually gave up on the regular practice of criticism was that the novels I was reading seemed to me less and less worth writing about. They might be more or less interesting, more or less amusing, but mostly they told me more about their authors, and less about life or the world, than I wanted or needed to know. Once upon a time the novel (as its English name suggests) had been a bringer of news; or (to put it in the terms you yourself use in your essay "The Novel and Europe") its mission had been to "uncover a hitherto unknown segment of existence." But novel after novel was now "only confirming what had already been said."

That is how you characterize the "hundreds and thousands of novels published in huge editions and widely read in Communist Russia." But "confirming what had already been said" was precisely what most of the novels written and published in the democratic West, including many honored for boldness and originality, were also doing. This was the situation twenty years ago, and it is perhaps even worse today. I do not, of course, mean that our novelists follow an official "party line," either directly or in some broader sense. What I do mean is that the most esteemed novels of our age in the West often seem to have as their main purpose the reinforcement of the by now endlessly reiterated idea that literary people are superior in every way to the businessmen, the politicians, the workers among whom they live—that they are more intelligent, more sensitive, and morally finer than everyone else.

You write, in the same essay from which I have just quoted, that "Every novel says to the reader: 'Things are not as simple as you think.'" This may be true of the best, the greatest, of novels. But it is not true of most contemporary American novels. Most contemporary American novels invite the reader to join with the author in a luxuriously complacent celebration of themselves and of the stock prejudices and bigotries of the "advanced" literary culture against the middle-class world around them. Flaubert could declare that *he* was Madame Bovary; the contemporary American novelist, faced with a modern-day equivalent of such a character, announces: How wonderful it is to have nothing whatever in common with this dull and inferior person.

In your essay on the novel you too bring up Flaubert, and you credit him with discovering "the *terra* previously *incognita* of the everyday." But what "hitherto unknown segment of existence" did you discover in *The Book of Laughter and Forgetting?* In my opinion, the answer has to be: the distinctive things Communism does to the life—most notably the spiritual or cultural life—of a society. Before reading *The Book of Laughter and Forgetting,* I thought that a novel set in Communist Czechoslovakia could "only confirm what had already been said" and what I, as a convinced anti-Communist, had already taken in. William Buckley quite reasonably asks: "How is it possible for the thousandth exposé of life under Communism to be original?" But what you proved in *The Book of Laughter and Forgetting* (and, I have since discovered, in some of your earlier novels like *The Joke* as well) is that it *is* possible to be original even in going over the most frequently trodden ground. You cite with approval "Hermann Broch's obstinately repeated point that the only *raison d'être* of a novel is to discover what can only be discovered by a novel," and your own novels are a splendid demonstration of that point.

If I were still a practicing literary critic, I would be obligated at this juncture to show how *The Book of Laughter and Forgetting* achieves this marvelous result. To tell you the truth, though, even if I were not so rusty, I would have a hard time doing so. This is not an easy book to describe, let alone to analyze. Indeed, if I had not read it before the reviews came out, I would have been put off, and misled, by the terms in which they praised it.

Not that these terms were all inaccurate. *The Book of Laughter and Forgetting* assuredly is, in the words of one reviewer, "part fairy tale, part literary criticism, part political tract, part musicology, and part autobiography"; and I also agree with the same reviewer when he adds that "the whole is genius." Yet what compelled me most when I first opened *The Book of Laughter and Forgetting* was not its form or its aesthetic character but its *intellectual force,* the astonishing intelligence controlling and suffusing every line.

The only other contemporary novelist I could think of with that kind of intellectual force, that degree of intelligence, was Saul Bellow. Like Bellow, you moved with easy freedom and complete authority through the world of ideas, and like him too you were often playful in the way you handled them. But in the end Bellow seemed always to be writing only about himself, composing endless and finally claustrophobic variations on the theme of Saul Bellow's sensibility. You too were a composer of variations; in fact, in *The Book of Laughter and Forgetting* itself you made so bold as to inform us that "This entire book is a novel in the form of variations." Yet even though you yourself, as Milan Kundera, kept making personal appearances in the course of which you talked about your life or, again speaking frankly in your own name, delivered yourself of brilliant little essays about the history of Czechoslovakia, or of music, or of literature, *you*, Milan Kundera, were not the subject of this novel, or the "theme" of these variations. The theme was totalitarianism: what it is, what it does, where it comes from. But this was a novel, however free and easy in its formal syncretism, whose mission was "to discover what can only be discovered by a novel," and consequently all its terms were specified. Totalitarianism thus meant Communism, and more specifically Soviet Communism, and still more specifically Communism as imposed on Czechoslovakia, first in 1948 by a coup and then, twenty years later in 1968, by the power of Soviet tanks.

Nowadays it is generally held that Communism is born out of hunger and oppression, and in conspicuously failing to "confirm" that idea, you were to that extent being original. But to anyone familiar with the literature, what you had to say about Communism was not in itself new: that it arises out of the utopian fantasy of a return to Paradise; that it can brook no challenge to its certainties; that it cannot and will not tolerate pluralism either in the form of the independent individual or in the form of the unique national culture.

All these things had been said before—by Orwell, Koestler, Camus, and most recently Solzhenitsyn. Indeed, according to Solzhenitsyn, Communism has done to Russia itself exactly what you tell us it has done to Czechoslovakia and all the other peoples and nations that have been absorbed into the Soviet empire. From the point of view of those nations it is traditional Russian imperialism that has crushed the life out of them, but in Solzhenitsyn's eyes Russia itself is as much the victim of Communism as the countries of Central Europe.

In another of your essays, "The Tragedy of Central Europe," you lean toward the perspective of the enslaved countries in fixing the blame on Russia rather than Communism, and you also agree with the great Polish dissident Leszek Kolakowski when he criticizes Solzhenitsyn's "tendency to idealize czarism." Nevertheless, there can be no doubt that *The Book of Laughter and Forgetting* is anti-Communist before it is anti-Russian. It begins not with Stalin but with the Czech Communist leader Klement Gottwald and the coup that brought Communism to power in Czechoslovakia, and you make it clear throughout that the utopian fantasies in whose service Czechoslovakia is gradually murdered as a nation come from within. It is only when the nation begins to awake and tries to save itself from the slow suicide it has been committing that the Soviet tanks are sent in.

Yet even though in one sense *The Book of Laughter and Forgetting* said nothing new about Communism, in another sense it "discovered" Communism as surely as Flaubert "discovered" everyday life (about which, after all, *Madame Bovary* said nothing new, either). As I have already indicated, I find it very hard to understand how you were able to make the familiar seem unfamiliar and then to familiarize it anew with such great freshness and immediacy. Perhaps the answer lies in the unfamiliar form you created, in which a number of apparently unrelated stories written in different literary genres, ranging from the conventionally realistic to the surrealistic, are strung together only by the author's direct intervention and a common theme which, however, is not even clearly visible in every case.

What, for example, connects Karel of Part II, who makes love simultaneously to his wife and his mistress as his aged mother sleeps in the next room, with Mirek of Part I, a disillusioned ex-Communist who gets six years in prison for trying to keep a careful record of events after the invasion of Czechoslovakia? Then there is the section about the student who rushes off to spend an evening getting drunk with a group of famous poets while a married woman he has been lusting after waits impatiently for him in his room. Why is the fairly straight comic realism of that section immediately followed by the grim Kafkaesque parable of the young woman who finds herself living in a world populated exclusively by little children ("angels") who at first worship and then finally torment her to death?

Whatever explanations subsequent analysis might yield, the fact is that those "brutal juxtapositions" make so powerful an effect on a first reading that they justify themselves before they are fully understood; and here too (at least so far as I personally was concerned) you prevailed against resistance. Nowadays my taste in fiction runs strongly to the realistic, and the enthusiasm I once felt for the experimental has waned as experimental writing has itself become both conventional and purposeless. But just as you have "discovered" Communism for the novel, so you have resurrected formal experimentation. The point of such experimentation was not originally to drive the novel out of the world it had been exploring for so long through the techniques and devices of realism; the point was to extend those techniques to previously unexplored regions of the inner life. What you say of Bartók, that he "knew how to discover the last original possibility in music based on the tonal principle," could be said of what Joyce, Kafka, and Proust were doing in relation to the fictional principle of verisimilitude. It can also, I believe, be said of you.

But since you yourself compare *The Book of Laughter and Forgetting* to a piece of music, it seems appropriate to admit that in reading it I was not so much reminded of other modern novelists as of the tonal modernist composers who, no matter how dissonant and difficult they may be (some of Bartók's own string quartets are a good case in point), are still intelligible to the ear in a way that the atonal and serial composers are not, no matter how often one listens to their works. Bartók, Stravinsky, Prokofiev, Shostakovich, and your beloved Janáček all found new and striking means by which to make the familiar world of sound seem new—to bring it, as we say, back to life. And this, it seemed to me, was what you were doing to a familiar world of experience in *The Book of Laughter and Forgetting*.

A few weeks after I had finished reading it, *The Book of Laughter and Forgetting* was published in the United States, and to my amazement the reviewers were just as enthusiastic about it as I had been. If you are wondering why this should have amazed me, I will tell you frankly that I would not have expected the American literary world to applaud so outspokenly anti-Communist a book. In France, where you have been living since 1975, anti-Communism may lately have come into fashion among intellectuals, but here in the United States it has for some years been anathema to literary people—and to most other people who think of themselves as liberals or as "sophisticated" or both. Very few of these people are actually sympathetic to Communism, but even fewer of them take it seriously as a threat or even as a reality. They are convinced that no one in the Soviet Union, let alone the satellite countries, believes in Communism any longer, if they ever did; and as for the Third World, the Marxist-Leninists there are not really Communists (even to call them Communists is taken as a sign of political primitivism) but nationalists making use of a convenient rhetoric. Hence to be an anti-Communist is to be guilty of hating and fearing an illusion—or rather, the ghost of something that may once have existed but that has long since passed away.

In the view of most American literary people, however, anti-Communists are not merely suffering from paranoid delusions; they are also dangerous in that they tend to exaggerate the dimensions of the Soviet threat. Here again, just as very few of these people are pro-Communist, hardly a single one can be found who is openly or straightforwardly pro-Soviet. Once there were many defenders of and apologists for the Soviet Union in the American literary world, but that was a long time ago. In recent years it has been almost impossible to find a writer or a critic who will argue that the Soviet Union is building a workers' paradise, or who will declare that Soviet domination of the countries of Central Europe is a good thing.

On the other hand, it is now the standard view that in its conflict with the West, or rather the United States, the Soviet Union is more sinned against than sinning. Everything the Soviets do (even the invasion of Afghanistan) is defensive or a reaction to an American provocation; and anything that cannot be explained away in these terms (the attempted assassination of the Pope, the cheating on arms-control agreements, the use of poison gas) is denied. The idea that seems self-evident to you (and to me), namely, that the Soviets are out to dominate the world, is regarded as too patently ridiculous even to be debated; it is dismissed either with a patronizing smile or with a show of incredulous indignation. One is permitted to criticize the Soviet Union as a "tyranny," but to see it as a threat is both to be paranoid and to feed Soviet paranoia, thereby increasing the risk of an all-out nuclear war.

Given this frame of mind, most reviewers might have been expected to bridle at the anti-Communism of *The Book of Laughter and Forgetting*. But none of them did. Why? Possibly some or even all of them were so impressed with your novel as a work of art that they were willing to forgive or overlook its anti-Communism. Perhaps. But in any event—and this is a factor I should have anticipated but did not—as a Czech who has suffered and is now in exile, you have a license to be anti-Soviet and even anti-Communist. All Soviet or Central European dissidents are granted that license. By sympathizing with and celebrating dissident or refugee artists and intellectuals from the Communist world, literary people here can demonstrate (to themselves as much as to others) that their hatred of oppression extends to the Left no less than to the Right and that their love of literature also transcends political and ideological differences.

If you ask me what objection I or anyone else could conceivably have to such a lofty attitude, I will ask you in turn to reflect on the price that you yourself are paying for being treated in this way. In a piece about the reaction in France to your latest novel, *The Unbearable Lightness of Being,* Edmund White writes: "When faced with a figure such as Kundera, French leftists, eager to atone for former Soviet sympathies, begin to echo the unregenerate anti-Communism of Gaullists." The opposite has been true of the American reaction to your work. Here it has either become yet another occasion for sneering at "unregenerate anti-Communism" or else it has been described in the most disingenuously abstract terms available. You are writing about memory and laughter, about being and nonbeing, about love and sex, about angels and devils, about home and exile—about anything, in short, but the fate of Czechoslovakia under Communism and what that fate means, or should mean, to those of us living in the free world.

Thus one of your leftist admirers in America assures us that "Kundera refuses to settle into a complacency where answers come easy; no cold-war scold he. He subjects the 'free world's' contradictions to equally fierce scrutiny; the issues he confronts—the bearing of time, choice, and being—transcend time and place." Neither, according to another of your admirers who also puts derisive quotation marks around the phrase free world, do you detect any fundamental difference between the fate of literature under conditions of artistic freedom and what happens to it under Communist totalitarianism: "His need to experiment with form is surely connected to his personal vendetta against the puerilities of 'socialist realism' and its 'free world' counterparts."

What is being done to you here, I have come to see, bears a macabre resemblance to what has been done posthumously to George Orwell. In Orwell's own lifetime, no one had any doubt that the species of totalitarianism he was warning against in *Nineteen Eighty-Four* was Communism. Yet as we have all discovered from the endless discussions of that book occasioned by the coming of the real 1984, it is now interpreted and taught more as a warning against the United States than the Soviet Union. If the word Orwellian means turning things into their opposites ("war is peace," etc.), then Orwell himself has been Orwellianized—not by an all-powerful state in control of all means of expression and publication, but by what Orwell himself called the "new aristocracy" of publicists and professors. This new aristocracy so dominates the centers in which opinion is shaped that it is able to distort the truth, especially about the past, to a degree that Orwell thought could never be reached so long as freedom of speech existed.

Like Orwell before you, you are obsessed with the theme of memory, and you believe with one of your characters "that the struggle of man against power is the struggle of memory against forgetting." The power you have in mind is the political power of the totalitarian state, but what the case of Orwell so ironically and paradoxically and poignantly demonstrates is that in the democratic West the power against which memory must struggle is the *cultural* power of the "new aristocracy." This power, with no help whatever from the state (and indeed operating in opposition to the state), has taken the real Orwell, to whom nothing was more fundamental than the distinction between the free world and the Communist world, and sent him down the memory hole, while giving us in his place an Orwell who was neutral as between the United States and the Soviet Union and who saw no important differences between life in a Communist society and life in the democratic West.

Now that same power is trying to do the same thing to you. But of course this is an even more brazen operation. Orwell's grave has been robbed; you are being kidnapped.

When I first thought of writing to you about this, I assumed that you would be appalled to learn how in America your work was falling into the hands of people who were using it for political purposes that you would surely consider pernicious. But now *I* am appalled to learn that you have been cooperating with your own kidnappers. "If I write a love story, and there are three lines about Stalin in that story," you tell the *New York Times Book Review,* "people will talk about the three lines and forget the rest, or read the rest for its political implications or as a metaphor for politics." But in America, once again, the opposite more nearly obtains: you write a book about Czechoslovakia under Communism containing three lines about love and everyone talks about those three lines and says that Czechoslovakia under Communism is a metaphor for life in the "free world" (in quotation marks of course). Or you write a novel, *The Unbearable Lightness of Being,* containing a brief episode in which an anti-Communist Czech émigré in Paris is seen by one of the characters as no different in kind from the Communists back in Prague (both being equally dogmatic), and virtually every reviewer gleefully cites it by way of suggesting that in your eyes Communism and anti-Communism are equivalent evils.

I think I can understand why a writer in exile from a

Communist society should wish to turn his back on politics altogether, particularly where his own work is concerned. It is, after all, the essence of totalitarianism to politicize everything, most emphatically including the arts, and what better protest could there be against this distinctive species of tyranny than to insist on the reality and finally the superior importance of the nonpolitical in life? You are, for example, obviously fascinated by erotic experience in its own right and for its own sake, and that is why you write about it so much. Yet it is hard to escape the impression that sex also plays such a large role in your novels because under Communism it became the only area of privacy that remained relatively intact when everything else had become politicized. (Surely too you make fun of orgies and nude beaches because they represent an effort to turn sex into a servant of the utopian fantasies that Communism has failed to satisfy.)

But even greater than your passion for sex is your love of Western civilization, and especially its literature and its music. If I read you correctly, nothing that Communism has done, none of the crimes it has committed, not even the Gulags it has created, seems to you worse than the war it has waged against Western culture. To you it is a war that goes beyond the stifling of free expression or the effort by the state to prescribe the very forms in which artists are permitted to work. It is *total* war. It involves the complete cultural annihilation by the Soviet Union of the countries of Central Europe, and this in turn—so you believe—represents the amputation of a vital part of Western civilization.

You make a powerful case in "The Tragedy of Central Europe" for the proposition that the countries of that area are "the cultural home" of the West. From this it follows that in acquiescing since Yalta in their absorption into the alien civilization of the East (alien because "Russian Communism vigorously reawakened Russia's old anti-Western obsessions and turned it brutally against Europe"), the West has shown that it no longer believes in the worth of its own civilization. The unity of the West was once based on religion; then religion "bowed out, giving way to culture, which became the expression of the supreme values by which European humanity understood itself, defined itself, identified itself as European." The tragedy of Central Europe has revealed that "Just as God long ago gave way to culture, culture in turn is giving way." To what? You do not say because you do not know. "I think I know only that culture has bowed out" in the West.

You do not explicitly add here that you for one are refusing to bow out, but you do tell us elsewhere that your supreme commitment is to the heritage of the European novel. You further give us to understand that as a novelist you mean to keep faith with your Central European heritage in particular—a heritage embodied in a "disabused view of history" and "the 'nonserious spirit' that mocks grandeur and glory." Summing it all up, you once responded to someone who had praised your first book as an indictment of Stalinism with the irritable remark: "Spare me your Stalinism. *The Joke* is a love story. . . . [It] is *merely* a novel."

Your love of culture, then, gives you a double incentive to deny the political dimension of your work. You wish to protect it from the "mindlessness of politicization," and at the same time to be antipolitical is a way of *not* forgetting the murdered spirit of Czechoslovakia and the other countries of Central Europe which have now "disappeared from the map."

Even though I do not share your generally sour attitude toward religion, to all this I say: Yes, yes, and again yes. But I ask you, I implore you, to consider that by cooperating with those who have kidnapped your work, you are "bowing out" yourself. The testimony of the dissidents behind the

Iron Curtain, whether they languish in prison or now live in the West, has played an immense role in forcing the intellectuals of Europe and America to think about the political values at stake in the conflict between East and West. Now you have come along and forced us all to begin thinking again (or perhaps for the first time) about the *cultural* dimension of this struggle. This has been the distinctive contribution, and the glory, of your work. Why then should you wish to encourage the agents of the very cultural abdication you deplore and mourn and lament? Why should you, of all writers, wish to be coopted by people who think there is no moral or political—or cultural—difference between West and East worth talking about, let alone fighting over? Why should you allow yourself to provide cover for people who think that Western civilization should not and cannot be defended?

You will perhaps answer in the words with which your essay on the novel concludes: "I am attached to nothing apart from the European novel," and that the "wisdom of the novel" requires skepticism as opposed to dogmatic certainty, the refusal to take sides, the raising of questions rather than the finding of answers. But let me remind you of what you also know—that the novel is devoted to exploring the concrete and the particular. Those on the American Left who have taken you up have been able to do so only by ignoring the novelistic essence of your work, its concreteness and its particularity: by robbing it (to adapt the guiding metaphor of your latest novel) of *weight,* by cutting it loose from the earth and letting it float high into a realm of comfortable abstractions in which all moral and political distinctions become invisible, and everything merges into "the unbearable lightness of being."

In the novel to which you give that phrase as a title, you profess uncertainty as to whether one should choose weight or lightness, but that novel itself, like your writing in general, belies the uncertainty. In your work you have chosen weight, which is to say the burdens of memory and the celebration of a "world of concrete living." Even your flirtation with the irresponsibilities of lightness paradoxically adds to that weight, deriving as it does from the heavy burden you have accepted of keeping the mocking and irreverent spirit of your culturally devastated homeland alive: a spirit that darkens the lightness of the laughter you so value and that throws the shadow of the gallows over the jokes you love to make.

You have declared in an interview that you want all of us in the West to understand what happened at Yalta, that it is necessary for "a Frenchman or an American . . . to know, to reason, to comprehend what is happening to, say, people in Czechoslovakia . . . so that his naiveté won't become his tragedy." It is for the sake of that necessary understanding that I beg you to stop giving aid and encouragement to the cultural powers who are using some of your own words to prevent your work from helping to alert a demoralized West to the dangers it faces from a self-imposed Yalta of its own.

9.

THE TERRIBLE QUESTION OF
ALEKSANDR SOLZHENITSYN

To think seriously about Aleksandr Solzhenitsyn—to immerse oneself in his work, to contemplate the story of his life—is such a hard thing to do, so unpleasant, so unsettling, that no one without a special reason is likely, once having started, to persist. The difficulty begins with the sheer quantity of Solzhenitsyn's work. Even omitting books that remain untranslated, and skipping over minor works of verse and drama, the English-language reader is still confronted with about five thousand pages, most of them closely printed, and all of them written with the kind of density that demands unflagging attention: if the mind wanders for so much as a few seconds when reading Solzhenitsyn, the thread is almost certain to be lost.

To compound the difficulty, Solzhenitsyn's very subject matter is guaranteed to induce a wandering mind. If he is not describing imprisonment under conditions of hunger, sleeplessness, and cold (or heat) that one would have thought too harsh to sustain life, let alone endless hours of grueling labor, then he is writing about the horrors of the battlefield, or the terrors of patients afflicted with cancer, or the humiliations and anxieties of writers working under the eye of semiliterate censors and KGB thugs. How is it possible to keep the mind from wandering in search of relief from so relentless an assault? And how, when it has rebelled by wandering, can it be brought back? *The Gulag Archipelago* is one of the most famous books ever written, but I know from asking that very few people have managed to get all the way through the six hundred pages of the first volume and that hardly any at all have read the even longer second and the only slightly shorter third.

As for Solzhenitsyn's novels, their readership, I would guess, again from asking, has declined with each succeeding one. The first (and the shortest), *One Day in the Life of Ivan Denisovich,* has been very widely read, but *The First Circle* and *Cancer Ward* have proved disappointing to many enthusiasts of *Ivan Denisovich,* while *August 1914* and *Lenin in Zurich* have, I believe, been more reviewed than read. Indeed, so far had the public mind wandered from Solzhenitsyn by 1980 that *The Oak and the Calf,* perhaps his most readable book, was hardly noticed when it was published in that year.

But of course by 1980 something had happened to Solzhenitsyn which placed between him and the Western reading public another and even greater obstacle than the length, the density, and the unpleasant subject matter of his books. He had become, to use the usual euphemism, "controversial." And thereby hangs a tale.

Before his expulsion from the Soviet Union in 1974, Solzhenitsyn had been seen in the United States, and in the West generally, as one of the two greatest and most heroic of the Soviet dissidents (the other being Andrei Sakharov). As such, he was also taken to be a "liberal"—which, in a certain sense and in the context of Soviet society, he undoubtedly was. On occasion he even called himself a liberal, meaning by this that he was fighting against the censorship of literature and the arts.

In those days, too, Solzhenitsyn was careful not to overstep certain limits in his challenge to the Soviet authorities. He had originally been arrested toward the end of World War II, while still in the army, when it was discovered that he had made disparaging jokes about Stalin; for this he had been sentenced to eight years in prison camps and another three in internal exile. Yet neither the fact that he was critical of Stalin, nor his bitterness over being imprisoned, at first turned Solzhenitsyn into an anti-Communist. He remained a Marxist and a Leninist in whose eyes Stalin had betrayed the revolutionary heritage of 1917. It was only in the Gulag that he gradually came to see Stalin and Stalinism not as the betrayal of Marxism and Leninism but as their logical culmination and fulfillment.

Having arrived at this realization, however, Solzhenitsyn prudently kept it to himself, even after Stalin's death and Khrushchev's de-Stalinization campaign. By posing as a Leninist who, like so many millions of other loyal Communists, had suffered unjustly for his premature opposition to the "cult of personality," Solzhenitsyn not only could aspire to rehabilitation as a Soviet citizen but could even hope that he might get away with a book that told the truth about Stalin's prison camps.

The strategy worked. *One Day in the Life of Ivan Denisovich* was submitted to the leading Soviet literary journal, *Novy Mir,* itself edited by just such a "liberal" Communist as Solzhenitsyn pretended to be, Aleksandr Tvardovsky (who was also Russia's most highly regarded living poet).

Thanks to Tvardovsky's maneuverings, publication of *Ivan Denisovich* was eventually authorized by Nikita Khrushchev himself; and in November 1962, literally overnight, an unknown forty-four-year-old ex-convict, employed as an elementary-school teacher of math and physics in a small provincial town, became one of the most celebrated writers on earth.

Nevertheless, after *Ivan Denisovich* and a couple of shorter pieces, *Novy Mir* rejected one manuscript after another by Solzhenitsyn—not because Tvardovsky disliked them but because, things having tightened up again, he feared that these manuscripts would be stopped by the censors and that the position of his magazine would thereby be jeopardized. Yet the false dawn of liberalization under Khrushchev had left a trace: these were the years when manuscripts, often copied in a feverish rush, were beginning to circulate through the clandestine network known as *samizdat* and were also being smuggled out of the Soviet Union and finding publishers in the West. It was via such channels that Solzhenitsyn's books came to light, simultaneously endangering him with the Soviet authorities and protecting him from their wrath. Taking shrewd advantage of this situation, Solzhenitsyn carried on a running battle with the Writers' Union, demanding that it stand up against the censorship of literature by insensitive party functionaries and appealing for support in getting his own novels published in the Soviet Union.

All this time, Solzhenitsyn was thought in the West (in the words of the appendix to the first British edition of *Cancer Ward* in 1968) to be "a loyal and patriotic Soviet citizen [whose] protests were directed against the bureaucracy's excesses and abuses, not against Soviet authority and the Communist society [and whose] aim was to improve and perfect the Soviet system, not to destroy it." And when, in 1970, Solzhenitsyn was awarded the Nobel Prize for literature, he was still the darling (to quote the appendix to *Cancer Ward* again) of "the liberal intellectuals of the West . . . the same people who had for years hoped for the liberalization of the Soviet state and worked hard for the reduction of East-West tensions."

About three years later, the KGB unearthed a hidden copy of *The Gulag Archipelago,* and Solzhenitsyn was finally arrested. But instead of being returned to prison as he had expected, he was stripped of his Soviet citizenship and deported to Germany. Now that he was in the West and beyond the reach of the KGB, Solzhenitsyn had no reason to continue posing as a good Communist fighting for his rights under Soviet law; dissembling would in any event have been impossible after the publication of *The Gulag Archipelago,* in which the origins of Stalin's terror are traced right back to Lenin himself and in which terror in general is seen as the essence of the Bolshevik Revolution. And in case his liberal admirers in the West should somehow fail to grasp the point, Solzhenitsyn proceeded to hammer it home in a series of speeches, interviews, and essays that left no room for doubt or ambiguity.

Evidently Solzhenitsyn's enemies in the Soviet Union had been right in calling him anti-Soviet and his apologists in the West had been wrong; and if it was treason for a Soviet citizen to be an anti-Communist, then Solzhenitsyn was indeed a traitor.

By itself being guilty of treason would not necessarily have damaged Solzhenitsyn's reputation in the eyes of the liberal intellectuals of the West. For one thing, many of them—as witness their attitude toward Alger Hiss, the Rosenbergs, Kim Philby, and Burgess-Maclean—saw nothing overwhelmingly reprehensible in treason. For another, the climate of opinion in the 1970s was very favorably disposed toward any individual defiance of authority in any country for any reason; dissent was the order of the day, never mind its content or direction. Angela Davis here, Solzhenitsyn there: it was all the same.

But Solzhenitsyn *here* turned out to be another story. For not only was he anti-Communist, he was antiliberal; and not only was he anti-Soviet, he was antidétente; and not only was he both antiliberal and antidétente, but he insisted on bringing the two antipathies together into a scathing denunciation of the West for its failure of nerve in the face of an ineluctable Communist threat. Here was a species of treason that the liberal intellectuals of the West were not quite so ready to forgive. "At one time," writes Michael Scammell in his biography of Solzhenitsyn, "one almost never heard a word against him; he was lionized and idolized"; but now "he is more often denounced as embittered or ignored as irrelevant."

Scammell disclaims any intention "to redress the balance," but the response to his book suggests that he has at least inaugurated a process of reconsideration. Not, to be sure, in all quarters. Thus the late Carl R. Proffer, a specialist in Soviet literature, in a review published in the *New Republic* just after his death, described Solzhenitsyn from beyond the grave as "an old man with the limited education of a convinced Soviet Leninist and the limited life of a totalitarian prisoner," an "amateur" whose work is marked by silliness and stupidity. It is all "claptrap," and yet "for two decades right-wing Russians and others tremblingly call him a prophet." More surprisingly, on the other hand, in such other liberal periodicals as the *Atlantic* (Bernard Levin), the *New York Review* (Aileen Kelly), and the *New York Times* (John Gross), Scammell's book has called forth pieces in

defense of Solzhenitsyn, none written by "right-wing Russians" and all leaning heavily on the word "prophet."

About Scammell's *Solzhenitsyn: A Biography,* there is bad
news and good news. The bad news is that it adds yet another thousand pages to the more than five thousand by
Solzhenitsyn himself that must be read by anyone wishing
to think seriously about him. The good news is that it is a
wonderful book, and not the least wondrous of its qualities
is that despite its daunting length it makes a serious encounter
with Solzhenitsyn easier rather than harder to undertake.

There is a great deal of autobiographical material in Solzhenitsyn's own books, especially the *Gulag* volumes and
The Oak and the Calf, but it is so disconnected and frag-
mentary that putting it all together into a coherent account
as one goes along is almost impossible. Thus even if Scammell had done nothing but this, his book would have performed a major service to anyone trying to think seriously
about Solzhenitsyn.

But Scammell does much more than merely organize Solzhenitsyn's scattered revelations about his own life into an
intelligible story; he also checks these occasionally tenden-
tious and self-serving revelations wherever possible against
other sources. Further, in addition to subjecting Solzhenitsyn's version of events to critical scrutiny, Scammell is critical of Solzhenitsyn's political ideas from his own unobtru-
sively expressed social democratic point of view. Yet the last
thing he wishes to do is "expose" or debunk Solzhenitsyn.
This is a book written out of the deepest respect for its subject, and it can be said of Scammell that as a biographer he
does what Matthew Arnold enjoined the critic to attempt to
do in dealing with a literary work: "To see the object as in
itself it really is."

Finally, Scammell is himself so good a writer that his
book is a pleasure to read. His prose is lucid and elegant; his

scholarship is scrupulous, well-digested, and lightly carried; and his narrative pace is steady and sure.

But if Scammell truly fulfills Matthew Arnold's injunction in dealing with Solzhenitsyn the man, he does not, in my opinion, do so well with Solzhenitsyn the writer, whom he seems to regard as a major artist in the line of the great nineteenth-century Russian novelists, in some respects resembling Tolstoy and in others Dostoevsky.

This view is very widely shared and is—or at least used to be—the foundation of Solzhenitsyn's enormous prestige. It was as a novelist that he burst upon the Soviet scene, it was as a novelist that he won the Nobel Prize, and it was as a novelist that the world held him in so high an esteem. It was also primarily as a novelist that Solzhenitsyn saw (and sees) himself. Indeed, one of the paradoxically surprising facts about Solzhenitsyn that emerges from Scammell's book is that he was always a literary man—surprising because when *Ivan Denisovich* was published in the West the impression was conveyed that its author was a scientist who had tried his hand at a novel as the best way to tell the world about Stalin's labor camps.

In fact, however, Solzhenitsyn had entertained literary ambitions all his life. "As a young child," says Scammell, "he had decided that he wanted to become one of three things: a general, a priest, or a writer." At the age of nine he was already writing stories, poems, and plays; at the age of thirteen he kept a journal called *The Literary Gazette;* and at the age of fifteen he wrote a novel. Even before reaching eighteen, he had resolved to write "a big novel about the Revolution" modeled on Tolstoy's *War and Peace,* and he even drafted a plan for it. All this time he was also immersing himself in the classics of Russian literature, reading and rereading the works of Pushkin, Gogol, Gorky, and especially Tolstoy. Nevertheless, he decided to study physics and mathematics at the university rather than literature, partly because it would be easier to make a living as a teacher of science.

Then, only days after his graduation, war broke out and Solzhenitsyn joined the army, becoming in due course an artillery officer. So much the writer was he by now that not even combat could stop him. While complaining in letters home that the continuous fighting at the front was keeping him from his "main work," he managed between battles to write several stories, and when he sent a batch of them off to two Soviet writers he admired, he announced to one of his friends that "I'll tear my heart out of my breast, I'll stamp out fifteen years of my life," if they should say that he had no talent.

If war could not stop Solzhenitsyn from writing, neither could imprisonment. In the Gulag, even on those rare occasions when pen and paper were available, to write was literally to risk one's life or at the very least to court more severe conditions and longer sentences. Yet even under those circumstances Solzhenitsyn went on writing, in his head if not on paper, and in verse rather than prose because verse was easier to memorize. In eight years he committed *tens of thousands* of lines to memory, and it was only after his release that he was able to transcribe them and even then only in secret.

A writer, then, from the very beginning and a literary man through and through. The ambitions of this writer, this literary man, moreover, knew virtually no bounds. Not only did he make grandiose plans like the one for a multivolume epic about the Bolshevik Revolution that would be nothing less than a successor to *War and Peace;* he also dreamed of rescuing and reviving the great traditions of Russian literature which were in danger of being forgotten and lost as a result of censorship and the state-imposed corruptions of "Socialist Realism."

It is a measure of Solzhenitsyn's almost incomprehensible single-mindedness that he should actually have stuck with the first of these ambitions, formed when he was only seventeen years old. The original scheme involved a Communist hero, and by the time he started work on the first volume (published here in 1972 as *August 1914*), he had undergone the revolution in his own political perspective that reversed his attitude both toward the Revolution (from positive to negative) and toward the Russia of the Czars (from negative to positive). Yet so little did this radical change in point of view affect the overall design that, according to Scammell, "he was able to incorporate some of the scenes written in Rostov nearly thirty years beforehand virtually without altering them."

Since *August 1914* has now been followed by several more volumes, of which only the excerpts concerning Lenin have thus far been translated into English (under the title *Lenin in Zurich*), with more yet to come, it is perhaps unfair to attempt a critical judgment. Nevertheless, it can already be said with confidence that if *August 1914* is a fair sample, *R-17* (as Solzhenitsyn calls this entire work-in-progress) has nothing in common with *War and Peace* except the superficial characteristics of length and theme.

War and Peace is about Russia during the Napoleonic wars and *August 1914* is about Russia during World War I; both move back and forth from the battlefield to the home front; and both contain fictional characters as well as historical personages. There, however, the resemblances end. *War and Peace,* one of the greatest of all novels, is alive in every detail, and *August 1914* is, to put it plainly, dead from beginning to end. Neither the fictional nor the historical personages are truly realized, and though the combat scenes are scrupulously rendered, they remain staged set pieces with no power to arouse the emotions or draw the reader in. As for the narrative line, it is driven by the grim energy of the author's will and not by the inner compulsion through which the living organism of a genuine work of novelistic art always unfolds itself.

In short, judging by *August 1914,* Solzhenitsyn's epic of the Revolution fails utterly in its claim to stand beside *War and Peace.* Beyond this, it bespeaks the collapse of the hope that Solzhenitsyn would rescue and revive the great stifled tradition of the nineteenth-century Russian novel.

It was this hope of a rebirth of Russian literature that was aroused in Tvardovsky and his colleagues on the editorial staff of *Novy Mir* when they read the manuscript of *One Day in the Life of Ivan Denisovich,* with its audaciously realistic exploration of life in a forced-labor camp. "They say that Russian literature's been killed," Tvardovsky exclaimed in the course of a drunken celebration over the anonymous manuscript that had been submitted to them. "Damn and blast it! It's in this folder. . . ." And when, finally, *Ivan Denisovich* was published, millions of Russians responded in much the same way. Scammell explains:

> It is hard for Westerners to grasp just how bleak and barren the Soviet literary scene is and was (especially in the early 60's), how parched and starving Soviet readers are for contemporary literature of any quality. . . . Paradoxically . . . although *Ivan Denisovich* was published in Moscow for avowedly political reasons and was received both there and abroad mainly as a political sensation, it was one of the few Soviet prose works since the war that could stand completely as a work of art and be discussed exclusively in terms of its aesthetic achievement, quite apart from its political qualities. It was a universal statement about the human con-

dition, and it was for this reason that comparisons were made with Tolstoy and Dostoevsky and that hungry readers cherished the book.

Yet, as Solzhenitsyn himself has often pointed out, and approvingly, Russian readers differ from Westerners in making little or no distinction between the aesthetic and the moral or spiritual dimensions of literature. Accordingly, it was not as "a universal statement about the human condition" that *Ivan Denisovich* was read and revered in the Soviet Union, but as a truthful rendering of a particular experience undergone by the Russian people.

This was naturally the case with former prisoners—*zeks*, to use the Russian term—who poured out their thanks to Solzhenitsyn in hundreds and even thousands of letters. Here are some examples: "My face was smothered in tears. . . . I didn't wipe them away or feel ashamed, because all this . . . was mine, intimately mine, mine for every day of the fifteen years I spent in the camps." Or again: "Although I wept as I read it, at last I felt myself to be an equal citizen with the rest. . . ." And again: "Thank you for your tremendous achievement, thank you from the bottom of my heart. I would give you anything, anything. Reading your story I remembered . . . the frosts and the blizzards, the insults and humiliations. . . . I wept as I read—they were all familiar characters. . . ."

Nor was it only former *zeks* who were grateful to Solzhenitsyn for *Ivan Denisovich*. "I kiss your golden hands," wrote one reader; "Thank you for your truthfulness," wrote another; "Thank you for your love and courage," said a third; and speaking for them all, one correspondent declared: "Thank goodness that you exist . . . look after yourself. Your existence is our happiness."

With the help of Scammell's brilliant account of the context, and by the exercise of a little imagination, a non-Russian can understand reactions such as these, even if he finds it impossible to share in them. For while *Ivan Denisovich* is certainly a better novel than *August 1914,* it never really rises to "a universal statement about the human condition," and no more than *August 1914* can it bear comparison with Tolstoy and Dostoevsky.

Yet Tvardovsky, going even further than mere comparison, pronounced *Ivan Denisovich* superior to Dostoevsky's *House of the Dead* because "there we see the people through the eyes of an intellectual, whereas here the intellectuals are seen through the eyes of the people." On this issue, however, even many admirers of *Ivan Denisovich* disagreed, asking why Solzhenitsyn had chosen to write from the point of view of a simple peasant instead of through the consciousness of an intellectual. Solzhenitsyn hotly defended himself against this criticism:

> Of course, it would have been simpler and easier to write about an intellectual (doubtless thinking of oneself all the while: "What a fine fellow I am and how I suffered"). But . . . having been flung together with [Ivan Denisovich] Shukhov in the same sort of conditions . . . a complete nobody as far as the others were concerned and indistinguishable from the rest of them . . . I had a chance to feel exactly the same as they.

Scammell, agreeing with Tvardovsky and Solzhenitsyn against the critics, adds that "By making his hero a common peasant, Solzhenitsyn was able to seize the essence of the labor-camp experience and universalize it. An intellectual hero would have been less typical and more particular, diluting the story's power and impact."

Surely, however, the impact of the story is weakened, not strengthened, by being told through a character whose life on the outside has been as full of hardship and deprivation as Ivan Denisovich Shukhov's, and who has therefore become so accustomed to the kind of conditions he is forced to endure in the labor camp that he can end a day of unrelieved horror in a state of happiness over all the luck he has had in not suffering even more ("They hadn't put him in the cooler. The gang hadn't been chased out to work in the Socialist Community Development. . . . They hadn't found that piece of steel in the frisk," and so on). Solzhenitsyn intended this conclusion as a celebration of the resiliency of the human spirit, and so it is. But at the same time it makes identifying with Ivan Denisovich Shukhov (or entering into his skin, to use Solzhenitsyn's image) almost insuperably difficult.

No such problem of identification is presented by *The First Circle,* which is set in the least harsh "island" of the Gulag, a prison (known as a *sharashka*) housing scientists whose forced labor takes the form of research on various projects useful to the state. Here, therefore, all the main characters are intellectuals and they spend a good deal of time arguing about philosophy, politics, and the history of their country.

In moving from the "inferno," as it were, of *Ivan Denisovich* to the *sharashka,* "the first circle" of this prison-camp hell, Solzhenitsyn was trying both to broaden and deepen his fictional exploration of the Gulag. *The First Circle* is thus very much longer than *Ivan Denisovich* and includes a much wider representation of Soviet society, ranging from Stalin himself through various levels of the party hierarchy and down to the depths of the prison system and its inhabitants. In *Ivan Denisovich,* we see Shukhov taking pride in the physical labor he is forced to do, and in *The First Circle* the prisoner-scientists are similarly fired up over a project that, if successfully completed, will enable the KGB to keep even closer surveillance over the population. The difference (tending to vindicate the critical view of *Ivan Denisovich*) is that for some of the characters in *The First Circle* this poses the kind of acute moral dilemma that lies far beyond the range of Shukhov's consciousness.

But if it is easier to identify with the characters in *The First Circle* than with Ivan Denisovich Shukhov, it is harder to sustain an interest in them over the course of this very long novel. As in *August 1914*—and as in *Cancer Ward,* another long and thickly populated novel set in a hospital for patients suffering from cancer—Solzhenitsyn doggedly does all the things a novelist is supposed to do. He constructs plots, he catalogues details of scene and character, he transcribes conversations, he sets up dramatic conflicts, he moves toward resolutions. Yet all to no avail. Edmund Wilson once said of F. Scott Fitzgerald that despite everything that was wrong with his novels they never failed to live. The opposite can be said of Solzhenitsyn's novels: despite everything that is right about them, they always fail to live.

In maintaining, however, that Solzhenitsyn is not a true novelist, let alone another Tolstoy or Dostoevsky, I am far from suggesting that he is not a great writer. On the contrary, in my opinion his two major nonfiction works, *The Gulag Archipelago* and *The Oak and The Calf,* are among the very greatest books of the age. Everything that he tries, and fails, to do in his novels is magnificently accomplished in these works. While the novels never come to life, there is so much vitality in the three volumes of *The Gulag Archipelago* that it threatens to overwhelm, and undermine, the horrors of the material. For never can such stories have been told with such verve, such gusto, such animation, such high-spirited irony and sarcasm as Solzhenitsyn brings to this history of the Soviet prison system.

But to call *The Gulag Archipelago* a history is a little like describing the Talmud as a legal encyclopedia. The reason the Talmud is so hard to describe to anyone unacquainted with it is that there is nothing else quite like it to which it can be usefully compared. The same thing is true of *The Gulag Archipelago*.

In the absence of archives or histories or other published sources, Solzhenitsyn's research at first consisted of collecting reports and stories from former *zeks*—227 of them, to be exact—through secret meetings and carefully concealed correspondence; only later did he have access to such published materials as existed in restricted library collections. Drawing on all these sources, and on his own experience as well, Solzhenitsyn managed, through concrete episodes, biographical and autobiographical detail, historical analysis, and an almost infinite variety of literary modes and devices, to reconstruct the entire history of the Soviet prison-camp system and to convey the experience of the many millions (as many as 100 million all told, he estimates) who lived and died on the "islands" of the "archipelago." Writing this book, especially under conditions of enforced secrecy, was a stupendous feat of mind, spirit, creative originality, and stamina. It will stand forever as one of the majestic achievements in the history of literature.

Solzhenitsyn himself valued *The Gulag Archipelago* highly enough to resolve that, if his children were kidnapped and held hostage by the KGB as a way of preventing him from authorizing its publication in the West, he would sacrifice them rather than permit the book to be suppressed. But to *The Oak and the Calf* (where we learn about this "superhuman decision" to choose *The Gulag Archipelago* over his own children) he ascribed very little importance indeed. He called it *"secondary* literature: literature on literature, literature apropos of literature, literature begotten by literature," and he apologized in a preface for wasting the reader's time with such inferior stuff: "So much has been written, and people have less and less time for reading: should we, in all conscience, be writing memoirs, and literary memoirs at that?"

The irony is that *The Oak and the Calf* is not only far superior to any of Solzhenitsyn's "works of primary literature" (by which he means his novels), but even exceeds them in the very qualities that are usually thought of as novelistic. For example, there is not a single character in Solzhenitsyn's novels as vividly and fully realized as the character of Aleksandr Tvardovsky in *The Oak and the Calf*. Nor does any of the novels carry the dramatic force— the drive, the pace, the suspense—of *The Oak and the Calf*. Somehow, in telling the story of his own literary career, Solzhenitsyn was able to make far better use of his novelistic skills than he ever could in the writing of actual novels. The result is a great work of autobiography, and one of the most revealing books ever written about life, and particularly cultural life, in the Soviet Union.

Solzhenitsyn is not the only writer in our time who has largely been valued both by himself and the world as a novelist but whose best work has been done in forms other than prose fiction. Norman Mailer and James Baldwin spring to mind immediately as American examples of this phenomenon. It goes without saying that Solzhenitsyn towers over writers like these, but he has in common with them a quasi-religious attitude toward art in the traditional sense: to be a writer means to compose novels, poems, or plays. These are what make up—in Solzhenitsyn's own terms—"primary literature"; everything else is "secondary." But whereas Mailer and Baldwin are merely writers who mistake the nature of their own true talents (encouraged in this by a culture that accords higher status to fiction than to nonfiction), Solzhenitsyn presents a more complicated problem. And it is in trying to grapple with that problem that we immediately run up against the much-vexed issue of Solzhenitsyn the prophet.

There can be no doubt that Solzhenitsyn has come in retrospect to regard himself as an instrument of the will of God. As is clear from many hints and suggestions in *The Oak and the Calf,* he believes that, unbeknownst to himself, he was appointed to rescue from oblivion "the millions done to death" in the Gulag. It was for this purpose that he was sent to the Gulag himself; it was for this purpose that he survived the ordeal; and it was also for this purpose that his life was spared once more after he developed a cancerous tumor that had been diagnosed as fatal. Not only did God mark him out and then spare him for this mission; God also (though, again, he was unaware of it at the time—there were no visions or voices from on high) guided his steps in his struggles with the Soviet authorities, enabling him, a lone individual, to defy the awesome power of a totalitarian state and live to tell the tale.

It is not necessary to accept Solzhenitsyn's interpretation of his own life, or even to share his belief in God, in order to understand how and why he should have come to see himself as an instrument of the divine will. Indeed, one measure of the greatness of *The Oak and the Calf* is that it makes this conviction of Solzhenitsyn's seem at the very least plausible and even a rationally irresistible conclusion from the clear evidence of his life. In any case, whether or not one believes in God, and whether or not one believes that Solzhenitsyn is an instrument of the divine will, *his* belief has produced those "clear effects" to which William James pointed as the "pragmatic" test of a genuine religious experience.

The first, and the grossest, of those effects is to have kept Solzhenitsyn alive when he might so easily have succumbed to the hardships of his years in the labor camps and then to his struggle with cancer. He himself takes the view that "People can live through hardship, but from hard feelings they perish," and that "Cancer is the fate of all who give themselves up to moods of bilious, corrosive resentment and depression." What saved Solzhenitsyn from such mortally dangerous "hard feelings" was his conviction that the millions done to death in the Gulag depended on him to rescue them from yet a second and in some ways an even more terrible death—the death of oblivion. If he weakened, if he faltered, if he himself were to die, they would all sink unremembered, unrecorded, into a silent pit.

Thus, reproaching himself for "the mistaken sense of obligation" that led him to follow Tvardovsky's advice that he hold back for a while after publication of *Ivan Denisovich,* Solzhenitsyn writes:

> Let me make myself clear. I did, of course, owe something to Tvardovsky, but the debt was purely personal. I had, however, no right to look at things from a personal point of view and to worry about what *Novy Mir* would think of me. My point of departure should always have been that I did not belong to myself alone, that my literary destiny was not just my own, but that of the millions who had not lived to scrawl or gasp or croak the truth about their lot as jail birds. . . . I, who had returned from the world that never gives up its dead, had no right to swear loyalty either to *Novy Mir* or to Tvardovsky. . . .

After the KGB had found and confiscated a hidden archive of his manuscripts, he reproached himself even more bitterly:

> Just one slip of the foot, one careless move, and my whole plan, my whole life's work, had come to grief. And it was

not only my life's work but the dying wishes of the millions whose last whisper, last moan, had been cut short on some hut floor in some prison camp. I had not carried out their behests, I had betrayed them, had shown myself unworthy of them. It had been given to me, almost alone, to crawl to safety; the hopes once held in all those skulls buried now in common graves in the camps had been set on me—and I had collapsed, and their hopes had slipped from my hands.

In these and similar passages, we see the apparently contradictory combination of megalomania and selflessness that come so miraculously together in the making of a true prophet. *Everything* depends on him alone, and yet he himself is nothing: truly nothing, a mere vessel. In the case of Solzhenitsyn, it is only keeping faith with the dead that keeps him alive, and more than alive: capable of feats of endurance, exertion, courage that do indeed seem "superhuman." This is a word he himself, as we have seen, uses in describing his decision to sacrifice his own children, if need be, rather than suppress *The Gulag Archipelago*. But I for one do not hesitate to apply it to the entire story of his life: to his survival, to his capacity for work, and to his defiance of the Soviet authorities. Nor, to repeat, is it necessary to see the hand of God in all this in order to recognize it as in some sense superhuman.

But even if one did see the hand of God in Solzhenitsyn's life, I do not think one would see it in his novels. Reading *War and Peace* or *Anna Karenina* one is hard put not to regard Tolstoy as superhuman; the young Maxim Gorky, for example, atheist though he was, could not help feeling that Tolstoy was more than a mere human being. But as a novelist, Solzhenitsyn is, one might say, all too human. In the making of novels, he is driven by ordinary and quite conventional literary ambitions. He wants to be a great artist and to write books worthy of the masters of Russian literature. The subject matter of those books is more or less the same as the subject matter of his nonfiction works, but the point, the overriding point, of the novels is to use it for the purposes of the author's artistic dreams and aspirations. In the novels, he is serving himself, he belongs to himself alone, his literary destiny is just his own. How do I know this? I know it from the simple fact that his novels are dead on the page, denied the breath of life that the novelist is only given the power to give when he is able to transcend himself and enter into the experience, the "skin," of others.

The opposite is true of Solzhenitsyn's nonfiction works. Again, the contrast with Tolstoy is instructive. Tolstoy, as we know from Henri Troyat's fascinating biography of him (a biography, incidentally, from which Tolstoy emerges looking like a character out of Dostoevsky), was certainly a megalomaniac, whether writing fiction or religious tracts. But it was only as a novelist that he became capable of self-lessness as well; the theoretically impossible marriage of these two opposing qualities in the writing of *War and Peace* and *Anna Karenina* is what makes them seem super-human. The Tolstoy who later wrote tracts and pamphlets was as little capable of selflessness as most human beings, even though it was this Tolstoy whom the world, with its usual perspicacity, took for a saint and a prophet.

With Solzhenitsyn the position is reversed. It is in *The Gulag Archipelago* and *The Oak and the Calf* that Solzhenitsyn's megalomania merges with selflessness. Here he *is* serving something more than the "purely personal." Here he does *not* belong to himself alone. Here his own "literary destiny" *is* beside the point. Here he *does* become a vessel through which "the millions who had not lived to scrawl or gasp or croak the truth about their lot" find voices and tongues and are at last able to tell what they know. And therefore, it is here, where he is true to his prophetic vocation, and here alone, that he also becomes a great writer.

As such he succeeds in accomplishing what he only imagines he is doing in and through his novels. To the Russian people he is returning their stolen or "amputated" national memory, reopening the forcibly blocked channels of communication between the generations, between the past and the present; and to other peoples in other parts of the world he is offering "the condensed experience" of his own country "accurately and concisely and with that perception and pain they would feel if they had experienced it themselves." To what end? Why, quite simply, to help them all avoid making the same mistake themselves: the mistake of submitting to Communism.

Here, then, we arrive at the very heart of Solzhenitsyn's prophetic mission: to preach against

> the failure to understand the radical hostility of Communism to mankind as a whole—the failure to realize that Communism is irredeemable, that there exist no "better" variants of Communism; that it is incapable of growing "kinder," that it cannot survive as an ideology without using terror, and that, consequently, to coexist with Communism on the same planet is impossible. Either it will spread, cancer-like, to destroy mankind, or else mankind will have to rid itself of Communism (and even then face lengthy treatment for secondary tumors).

It is by preaching so radically anti-Communist a point of view—and in terms allowing for no hope of negotiation or compromise and seeming to threaten another world war—that Solzhenitsyn has made himself more and more unpopular in the West. I am well aware that Solzhenitsyn's Western critics also include a number of staunch anti-Communists who oppose him not because he is a "cold warrior" but because he espouses a species of Russian nationalism that is explicitly antidemocratic and (so they claim) implicitly anti-Semitic. Indeed, several such critics have charged that the latest volume of *R-17*, which has not yet been translated into English, goes beyond implicit into open anti-Semitism in its recounting of the assassination of Stolypin, Czar Nicholas II's prime minister, by a terrorist of Jewish origin.

Others to whom I have spoken disagree, and not having read the book in question, I cannot make a firsthand judgment. But my own impression, based on an acquaintance with virtually everything by Solzhenitsyn that has been translated into English, and confirmed by Scammell's characteristically scrupulous examination of the question, is that the charge of anti-Semitism rests almost entirely on negative evidence. That is, while there is no clear sign of positive hostility toward Jews in Solzhenitsyn's books, neither is there much sympathy. I can well imagine that in his heart he holds it against the Jews that so many of the old Bolsheviks, the makers of the Revolution that brought the curse of Communism to Russia, were of Jewish origin; and in general he also seems to ignore the mordant truth behind the old quip (playing on the fact that Trotsky's real name was Bronstein) that "the Trotskys make the revolutions, the Bronsteins pay the bill." Still, whatever there may be in his heart, there is no overt anti-Semitism in any of his translated works.

There is also this to consider: that Solzhenitsyn has always defended Israel, even to the point of invidiously comparing the courage of the Israelis in the face of their Arab enemies with the appeasement of the Soviet Union by the Western democracies. To be sure, there was a time when it was possible for an anti-Semite to be a Zionist of sorts: the founder of Zionism himself, Theodor Herzl, thought that the anti-Semitic European governments would welcome the establishment of a Jewish state precisely because it would be a good way of getting the Jews out of Europe. But in our own day, Israel has become *the* touchstone of attitudes toward the Jewish people, and anti-Zionism has become the main and most relevant form of anti-Semitism. So much is this the case that almost anything Solzhenitsyn may think about the role of Jews in the past—or even in the post-Communist Russia of his dreams—becomes academic by comparison.

On the other hand, in contrast to his references to the Jews, Solzhenitsyn's speeches and pamphlets are full of overt attacks on the democratic West, whose loss of "civic courage" and whose capitulation to the "Spirit of Munich" ("concessions and smiles to counterpose to the sudden renewed assault of bare-fanged barbarism") he blames on secularism, materialism, and liberalism. It is this, rather than any intimations of anti-Semitism, on which Solzhenitsyn's liberal critics have fastened in trying to write him off. And even to some of us who agree with him about Communism and about the "Spirit of Munich," Solzhenitsyn's brand of Russian nationalism with its authoritarian coloration and its anti-Semitic potential presents the most unpleasant and the most unsettling facet of a serious encounter with his life and his work.

In my opinion, however, we who agree with Solzhenitsyn about Communism would be making the worst of mistakes if we allowed ourselves to join with his critics in dismissing him as a crank or if we ourselves were to ignore him as an embarrassment. His challenge to the Russian people is to liberate themselves from Communism by means of their own spiritual resources and without the help of the West, but no matter how we feel about the form of society he urges upon them in the post-Communist Russia for which he prays, *our* main business is with his challenge to *us*.

For here—it cannot be repeated too often—is a lone individual who, by having successfully stood up to the full power of the Soviet state, has made himself into a living reproach to the West: a parable in action of the very courage in the face of Communist totalitarianism that the West has been unable or unwilling to summon in its own dealings with the Soviet state. Solzhenitsyn's terrible and terrifying question to us is this: is it possible that courage like his own is all that we require to escape from the fate he has come to warn us against? Is it possible that the courage first to see the truth about Communism and then the correlative courage to act upon it can guide our steps to safety as his own courage guided Solzehenitsyn's, that it can make the Soviet leaders back down and ultimately, perhaps, even collapse, just as they did when confronted by Solzhenitsyn himself?

Forcing us to face that terrible question, rubbing our noses in it, has been Solzhenitsyn's prophetic mission to the West. To seize upon the antidemocratic Slavophilia of his message to the Russian people, or even his resentment of the Jews, as an excuse for continuing to evade the challenge of his life and his work would only confirm the worst of his charges against us—the charge that we are cowards. And it would bring us ever closer to the day when we too might find ourselves plunged headlong into that pit out of which Solzhenitsyn once clawed his way so that the dead might be remembered and the living might be saved.

INDEX

211

ABOUT THE AUTHOR

Norman Podhoretz has been the editor of *Commentary* magazine since 1960. His writings have appeared in most major publications in the United States as well as in other countries throughout the world. Mr. Podhoretz's previous books include *Why We Were in Vietnam* (1982), *The Present Danger* (1980), *Breaking Ranks: A Political Memoir* (1979), *Making It* (1967), and *Doings and Undoings: The Fifties and After in American Writing* (1964). He lives in Manhattan with his wife, Midge Decter.